NOT NECESSARILY STONED, BUT BEAUTIFUL

The making of
Are You Experienced

Sean Egan

Published by Unanimous Ltd
12 The Ivories, 6–8 Northampton Street, London N1 2HY

Series editor: Nicola Birtwisle
Text editor: Ian Fitzgerald

ISBN: 1 903318 54 8

Printed in China

4 5 6 7 8 9

Picture credits
Picture section page 1: Michael Ochs Archives/Redferns. 2 top: Rex Features; bottom: Petra Niemeier/Redferns. 3 top: Schmitz/Rex Features; bottom: Glenn A. Baker/Redferns. 4 top left and right: Harry Goodwin/Rex Features; bottom: Jan Olofsson/Redferns. 5: Rex Features. 6 top: Schmitz/Rex Features; bottom: Pictorial/Strange Things. 7 top: Michael Ochs Archives/Redferns; bottom: Barry Peake/Rex Features. 8 top left and right: Michael Ochs Archives/Redferns; bottom: Bob Baker/Redferns. 9 top: Michael Ochs Archives/Redferns; bottom: Schmitz/Rex Features. 10: Michael Ochs Archives/Redferns. 11 top: Harry Goodwin/Redferns; bottom: Pictorial Press. 12: Harry Goodwin/Redferns.

contents

introduction

LISTENING TO *ARE YOU EXPERIENCED* (the correct title: neither the U.S. nor U.K. version of the album title included a question mark) even 35 years after its release is awe-inspiring: classic song snapping on the heels of classic song; breathtaking guitar playing; sublime songwriting; the sheer rip-roaring power of the Jimi Hendrix Experience as a group. Imagine, then, how it was to audiences in 1967, when its aesthetic brilliance was matched, in a double whammy punch, with its sheer newness.

For what had ever sounded like *Are You Experienced* before? Prior to its May 1967 U.K. release, everything in rock had only hinted at what this album achieved. There had been abrasive hard rock such as "You Really Got Me," but nothing in the pulverizing league of "Manic Depression." There had been deployment of feedback, but only either as a cute gimmick ("I Feel Fine") or as an atonal symbol of rebellion ("My Generation"); never had it been used as it was in "Love or Confusion"—as a form of coloring every bit as valid as conventional musical sounds. That track, "Love or Confusion," had a dazzlingly surreal air about it that may have had a kind of precursor in the Beatles' "Tomorrow Never Knows," but also cranked it up a hundred notches. There had been guitar virtuosity before, but nothing compared with the blurred-handed technique in "Red House." It was clear that things were never going to be the same again.

What makes *Are You Experienced*'s artistic triumph mind-boggling is the preposterously piecemeal way in which the album was constructed. Rather than being the result of a conventional period of concentrated work, it was recorded in short sessions between gigs—gigs that were necessary to bring money into a setup that was sometimes dependent on Hendrix's manager/producer Chas Chandler selling the bass guitars he had played in the Animals. Often, the band would go into a studio on the same day they'd appeared on a live show or recorded a television or radio appearance. Almost every basic track of each song was perfected in one session. Furthermore, this wasn't a case of a band producing studio versions of songs they had honed in rehearsal: most of the songs on the album were shown by Hendrix to the band only at the start of the day's recording.

Though it is the quintessential studio album in that not a single track on it was either played live or rehearsed before it was recorded (discounting "Hey Joe," a feature of the American edition) and in that it boasted effects and layering of sounds beyond replication on stage, in a sense, *Are You Experienced* was not made in the studio at all, but merely achieved resolution there. From Hendrix's growing celebrity among his peers in London and the Experience acquiring a group cohesiveness through grotty little gigs in insalubrious corners of the United Kingdom to the process of Hendrix absorbing the resplendent pop and psychedelic music and philosophy of London into his existing R & B and blues outlook and Hendrix's domestic scenarios with lover and sometime muse Kathy Etchingham—all of these things contribute to the sounds, textures, and lyrics of *Are You Experienced*. They also took up far more time in the band's lives than did the perfunctory mechanics of laying down the tracks. Such was the alchemy of the Experience as an ensemble that visits to the studio seem merely to have been a matter of the physical presence required in order to take a snapshot of the band's perpetually inspired state.

As hinted at above, there are two *Are You Experienced* albums. When the album was released in the United States four months after its British appearance, it had a very different track listing from the U.K. original, as detailed below:

U.K. Edition: Are You Experienced

Side 1

Foxy Lady
Manic Depression
Red House
Can You See Me
Love or Confusion
I Don't Live Today

Side 2

May This Be Love
Fire
3rd Stone from the Sun
Remember
Are You Experienced

U.S. Edition: Are You Experienced

Side 1

Purple Haze
Manic Depression
Hey Joe
Love or Confusion
May This Be Love
I Don't Live Today

Side 2

The Wind Cries Mary
Fire
Third Stone from the Sun (*sic*)
Foxey Lady (*sic*)
Are You Experienced? (*sic*)

Reprise Records had jettisoned "Can You See Me," "Remember," and "Red House" in favor of the U.K. singles "Hey Joe," "Purple Haze," and "The Wind Cries Mary," shuffled the running order of the remainder and even changed the spelling and punctuation of titles, an example of the corporate arrogance and philistinism that was standard among American record companies at the time. It would be absurd, however, to discount the American *Are You Experienced* album. For three decades, that version was the only one that millions upon millions of Americans knew: it formed the American perception of Hendrix as an artist. Accordingly, this book treats the U.S. and U.K. versions as a sort of conflated release—rather in the way that the 1997 CD reissues do, by presenting all the tracks from both the U.K. and U.S. albums (except "Red House," a different version of which appears, farcically, on the U.S. CD), with the three singles' B-sides tagged on as bonus tracks.

This book is neither a biography (although Hendrix's circumstances and relationships are touched on where relevant) nor a career overview (although it does seek to provide a context for the album's recording by looking at what Hendrix had—or, rather, hadn't—achieved hitherto). There are many other books on Hendrix that do fit those criteria, some of which are listed in the bibliography. This book, instead, is concerned with the preparation, the recording, the marketing, and the impact of *Are You Experienced*—on the quite simple grounds that an entire book is justified when discussing what is clearly one of the greatest albums ever made.

before the Experience

"I DON'T THINK THAT JIMI WOULD ever have made it in America had he not come here first and formed the Experience. When they went back to the States they'd already become stars here, which made it easier. If he was just on his own over there and he'd never have come here and hadn't got a group, I think he'd never have been discovered. Nobody knows whether he would or he wouldn't but the fact of the matter is he'd been playing long enough and hadn't."

These are the words of Kathy Etchingham, the woman Jimi Hendrix met on his first night in London in 1966 and who became the major love interest of Hendrix's life. She is referring to the fact that, despite his incredible talent, Jimi Hendrix had achieved nothing truly substantial in his career until Chas Chandler discovered him and took him over to Britain to make him a star. By then, Hendrix was nearly 24 years old. His career in his homeland had been dogged by missed opportunities and bad luck, so much so that the various musical adventures in which he took part before the recording of *Are You Experienced* must, in their mediocrity and modesty, comprise the most inauspicious preamble to a classic album there ever was.

Hendrix was born on November 27, 1942, to a negligent mother, Lucille, while his father Al was on army duty overseas. Jimi was originally registered under the name Johnny Allen Hendrix. Following the departure of Lucille with a man with whom she was romantically involved, Hendrix was cared for by friends and relatives until his father returned home and claimed him. "I don't think he was very, very close to his family at all," says Etchingham. "He enjoyed seeing them when he went back and everything, but he wasn't close like a child would be to an extended family they were all part of. The only one he ever mentioned to me was somebody called Celestine, whom he'd lived with in California." As for Hendrix's relationship with his father, Etchingham reveals, "He hadn't even met his dad until he was over three years old, and the first thing his dad did when he went down to California is to get him on the train and then give him a good old beating to show him who's boss, so that gives you some indication of their relationship."

Al renamed the boy James Marshall Hendrix, although he was henceforward referred to as Jimmy. Jimmy Hendrix's first instrument was a harmonica, which he played when he was about four. He then played violin for a period. It's unclear whether he owned either instrument and for how long he worked at them, although the fact that he never played either during his exotic musical explorations toward the end of his life indicates that these were simple childhood dalliances. "Then I started digging guitars," he later recalled. "Every house you went into seemed to have one lying around." Every house except Hendrix's. Buying Jimmy a guitar was not an option for Al, even had he been so inclined. Hendrix's childhood was extraordinarily impoverished. As well as being a single parent, Al Hendrix was further financially hampered by his occupation of gardener, which was a seasonal job. At one point, circumstances were so bad that Al had to temporarily place Jimmy's younger brother Leon with foster parents. Al Hendrix found it difficult to accommodate the musical ambitions his young son started to harbor. "Discouraged it completely," says Etchingham. Nonetheless, Etchingham reveals, it was through his father that the teenage Jimmy acquired the instrument of his desires: "Jimi said his dad was playing cards with some other old bloke who had a guitar and Jimi was playing with the guitar, and the guy said, 'If you win, your son can have the guitar for five dollars,' or something like that. That's how he got the guitar."

Although Hendrix later admitted he had lost his passion for the guitar not long after starting to play it, his interest was reawakened by Chuck Berry, and, although he had the same teething problems as did fellow leftie Paul McCartney, Hendrix worked hard on the instrument. Once his imagination had been fired up by Berry—and once he'd learned that, as a lefthanded player, he needed to reverse the order of the strings—he practiced incessantly. Spurning instruction manuals, he learned six chords and six inversions from friend Lacy Wilbon and took it from there. His relentless "plunk, plunk, plunking"—to quote Al—was assisted by a keen ear, and he would have riffs and chord sequences memorized after just a few tries.

In junior high school, Jimmy played with schoolmates in a band called the Velvetones, which covered material by the likes of the Coasters. He was dismayed to find that his instrument was drowned out by his colleagues' playing. At some point in 1959, Al's attitude toward Jimmy's musical ambitions evidently softened (and his financial situation improved), as he bought Jimmy his first electric guitar, a Supro Ozark 1560S. This helped rectify Jimmy's problem: electrified, he was inaudible no longer.

Hendrix maintained his musical pursuits when he volunteered for the army in 1961. It was while in the 101st Airborne Division that Hendrix met Billy Cox, a bassist whom Hendrix would ultimately employ in the Band of Gypsys. It was Cox (who was discharged two months after an ankle injury caused the premature end of Hendrix's own army life) who got Hendrix his first taste of recording when he landed him a gig doing session work for Starday-King in November 1962. The session producer ended up mixing Hendrix's guitar out of the recordings (which have never surfaced since) because he was overpowering everybody else.

Hendrix began taking work as a backup man where he could get it. Among the relatively big names with whom he acquired gigs were Slim Harpo, the Marvelettes, and Curtis Mayfield and the Impressions. Hendrix decided to try his luck in New York. There, he would make his first proper recordings, albeit as a backing man. In 1963, he recorded several songs at Abtone Studios for Lonnie Youngblood, a saxophonist, vocalist, and songwriter specializing in what was then still called R & B but that was in reality something more akin to soul.

"I had just come out of the army and I was looking for some work," recalls Youngblood. "Hendrix was working with a friend of mine named Curtis Knight. They found out I was home from the service and they wanted a saxophone player, so Curtis hired me. First of all, I wasn't gonna work with Curtis Knight because Curtis Knight wasn't a great musician, but he told me he had this great guitarist named Jimmy James who was working with him. When I heard the band and I heard Jimmy, I said, 'Ah hell, I'd love to play with this guy.'

So I started playing with Curtis. We were working all over the city."

The pseudonym Hendrix had adopted was a tip of the cap to his main guitar hero. "See, he liked Elmore James a lot," explains Youngblood. "He liked all the guys a lot. He was a guitar fanatic. He liked all different people, but I think he had this thing about Elmore James 'cos he took his name." Elmore James (1918–1963) was a bluesman who was prolific neither as a recording artist (his stop–start career didn't get underway until he was into his thirties, and was subsequently hindered by ill health) nor as a songwriter (he tended to popularize the songs of others, particularly Robert Johnson, whom he had known). James was, however, hugely influential in slide, or bottleneck, guitar playing. Interestingly, his tendency toward massive amplification and distortion predated Hendrix's own experiments in those areas.

Not that Youngblood knew at the time that "James" was Hendrix's pseudonym. "And we knew a lot about each other—we talked a lot. We were good friends." That he could become so close to his new colleague and not even know his birthname is something Youngblood attributes to Hendrix's shyness: "He wasn't much of a guy who could talk. The way he was and the way he played the guitar was two different people."

The work the band was getting was threatened by Knight's idiosyncrasies: "Curtis was a nice guy and everything, [but] he couldn't really play, plus he had other interests," says Youngblood. "Curtis was like a ladies' man. He was like a pimp. So it interfered sometime with the little business we had. I said, 'Well, I'm splitting.' Naturally, the whole band wanted to go with me. I was already established as a band leader in Harlem. I could get plenty of work. It was great for me 'cos I had a ready-made band, so I took them with me.

"Then I started recording because I've always been in and out of studios, doing my own sessions. Jimmy didn't have no amplifier, so I had to go out myself and buy Jimmy an amp." The investment in Hendrix paid off. "It's always good playing with somebody that can really make you feel good on the job," Youngblood recalls with enthusiasm. "He was more effective, because he was probably more confident. Jimmy played the hell out of what he know. Jimmy knew quite a bit." Was he the best guitarist Youngblood had ever heard? "I would say he was damn near. Before that, I had backed up Chuck Berry. Chuck was a master, don't get me wrong, but Jimmy had the edge of Chuck because Jimmy could do more. He had more colors, he could do more stuff than Chuck. Jimmy could play a ballad as pretty as damn near Wes Montgomery."

Hendrix's energies at this point seem to have been focused entirely on playing. "He sung some Lee Dorsey songs and a few things, maybe some Muddy Waters, but he wasn't into singing," says Youngblood. Nor was his colleague interested in composition, although Youngblood says, "Certain things I wrote, he would have some suggestions."

Youngblood's music was actually rather pleasant soul—the slinky "She's a Fox" being particularly easy on the ear—but, in truth, is mainly only noteworthy today because of the presence of a certain budding genius. Hendrix's role in Youngblood's music was, of course, limited: what with soul's brass parts and its chinka-chinka guitar conventions, there was little room for the type of guitar virtuosity Hendrix was capable of. Nevertheless, that an extraordinary talent was in attendance at these sessions is patently obvious at several junctures in the recordings. The blurred-hand flourish in the introduction to "Go Go Shoes" is in no way an average piece of playing. Hendrix's guitar playing throughout "She's a Fox" evinces the fatness and larger-than-life sound of the Experience: in some places, his playing is uncannily like his work on "Little Wing" from the second Experience album, *Axis: Bold As Love*. Buyers should beware of other Hendrix-less Youngblood recordings, which were later overdubbed without Youngblood's knowledge by a Hendrix soundalike.

Confusion surrounds Hendrix's next recording venture, which occurred in March 1964 on the opposite coast. Arthur Lee—who sings backup on it—claims that "My Diary" is one of his compositions. Rosa Lee Brooks, Hendrix's lover and colleague in an Ike and Tina Turner–style act called Jimmy & Rose, says she wrote most of the lyric and Hendrix wrote the melody. (The song's intro, she says, is almost identical to that of "One Rainy Wish" from *Axis: Bold As Love*.) The record was released in mid-1965 on local label Revis along with a B-side, improvised by Hendrix on the day of recording, called "Utee."

By then, Hendrix had left Los Angeles and Brooks and was moving onto bigger things, having been offered a role in the backing band of the Isley Brothers, whose "Twist and Shout" had been a Top Twenty national hit in 1962 and, even more lucrative, had recently been covered by the Beatles. The Isley Brothers generously allowed Hendrix to become a star of the show, giving him longish solos and indulging his showmanship, which was already leading him to play guitar with his teeth. In addition, Hendrix got to record with the act. As well as on Isley Brothers recordings including "Testify," "The Last Girl," and "Looking for a Love," Hendrix played on "Have Mercy Baby" by Don Covay and the Midnighters in this period and, possibly, on said act's album *Funky Yo-Yo*.

Toward the end of 1964, Hendrix suffered one of his periodic bouts of weariness of dancing to another act's tune and left the Isley Brothers. Around the same time, he sought out Booker T & the MG's guitarist and studio arranger Steve Cropper but, though they jammed for several hours, nothing came of the meeting. The next significant time Cropper ran into Hendrix was at the Monterey International Pop Festival, where Cropper was playing with Otis Redding and Hendrix was about to launch himself into global superstardom.

Hendrix's next significant career move was playing guitar for '50s rock 'n' roll legend Little Richard, who, like the Isley Brothers, also allowed him to display the various tricks that were becoming part of his stage personality, including performing extravagant solos, playing behind his back, and playing with his teeth. This in some way alleviated Hendrix's resentment at having to pay fines for his long hair and his frilly shirts. During his time with Little Richard, Hendrix went by the name Maurice James. The only known recordings of Hendrix with Little Richard took place in early 1965 at an unidentified Los Angeles studio: "Dancing All Around the World" (also known as "Dance a Go-Go") and "I Don't Know What You've Got But It's Got Me." The latter was released as a single and reached number 92 in the U.S. Hot 100. As with Youngblood's recordings, there are also several fraudulent Little Richard recordings on the market that feature an overdubbed Hendrix imitator.

In mid-1965, Hendrix either quit or was fired from (depending on whom you believe) Little Richard's band. He subsequently rejoined the Isley Brothers, playing gigs with them and recording two sides of a single in Atlantic Studios on August 5, 1965: "Move Over Let Me Dance" and "Have You Ever Been Disappointed."

In July of that year, Hendrix had signed a contract with Sue Records and Copa Management of New York City, but nothing seems to have resulted from it. A somewhat more meaningful contract was the one Hendrix agreed to on October 15, 1965, with PPX Enterprises, run by one Ed Chalpin. Chalpin later claimed that in his 40 years as a producer and manager, Hendrix had been one of only eight people he considered special enough to sign. Lonnie Youngblood was well acquainted with Chalpin. "Ed had this studio," the saxophonist says. "Then he started doing things and making a lot of copy records: records that sounded like a record, making a hit because you're re-releasing it on somebody's name." As can be imagined from Youngblood's explanation of Chalpin's *modus operandi*, the recording work Chalpin secured for the very special guitarist he'd discovered doesn't seem to indicate particularly grand plans for him. In late 1965, Hendrix played guitar on "Suey," a track that would be the B-side of a Jayne Mansfield single. Another act Chalpin also produced and licensed recordings by was a new permutation of Curtis Knight and the Squires. Knight, obviously harboring no grudges, asked Hendrix to record with him, and Hendrix accepted. Hendrix would also subsequently resume live work with Knight. The resulting recordings, which took place during late 1965 and early 1966, constitute Hendrix's most substantial—in terms of numbers, not quality—pre-stardom recordings. (They are not to be confused with recordings from the summer of 1967, which were informal jams recorded when Jimi—by then a star—dropped by to see his old friend.) Knight seems to be a nice guy—he gave an instrument-less Hendrix a guitar as a present after being knocked out with his playing on their first meeting—but his material is embarrassingly generic where it's not plagiaristic. "Gotta Have a New Dress" has some merit, but the rest of this material is distinguished only by the occasional quicksilver solo or distinctive flourish from Hendrix. The live recordings Hendrix made with Knight in this period are a little more interesting, particularly for the way they reveal Hendrix to be an important part of the act (he sings many of the numbers). The Knight recordings were most recently issued on CD by the British label Jungle Records under the names *Knock Yourself Out* (studio) and *Drivin' South* (live).

Chalpin has said he would have recorded more material with Hendrix, but the guitarist abruptly disappeared. The next time he heard of his former client, Hendrix already had several hit singles in the United Kingdom. Chalpin started legal proceedings over the unauthorized recording of the man he had under exclusive contract, and was eventually paid off in the form of an entire album: *Band of Gypsys*.

Youngblood is skeptical about Chalpin having had genuine ambitions for Hendrix. "If he was signed with him—signed with him to do what?" he says. "Because he sure wasn't gonna put no record on him. If you sign to a studio or to somebody to record you and you ain't got no record out, that's sort of weird, ain't it?" Asked if Chalpin understood how talented Hendrix was, Youngblood replies, "No, no, no. I don't think he understood how talented nobody was. Whether he took somebody people really raved over and he got a break over, I think that was the determinant factor for him." As to the question of whether Chalpin could have turned Hendrix into a superstar the way Chas Chandler did, Youngblood is contemptuous: "Hell, no. That's out of the *ground*. That's out of the question. Completely out of the question."

In December, Les Paul, the inventor of the solid body electric guitar, saw Hendrix perform at a nightclub in Lodi, New Jersey. He later recounted that he'd never seen a guitarist so "radical." Unfortunately, Paul was en route to New York to drop off some master recordings and couldn't stay to speak to the guitarist. He made strenuous efforts to trace him afterwards, with no luck. The following January, Hendrix joined the King Curtis All Stars. He stayed with the band, named after the saxophonist famous for his work on Coasters records, for about six months and took part in several recording sessions with them, including "Help Me" (Parts 1 & 2). An unconfirmed Hendrix studio role from that year is "I'm So Glad," recorded by Frank Howard and the Commanders.

In May 1966, Hendrix was playing gigs in New York with Curtis Knight. Model Linda Keith was staying with friends in New York while her boyfriend, Keith Richards, toured with the Rolling Stones. Stopping into a club called the Cheetah one evening, she caught a show by Knight but was far more interested in one of his backing men. "It was like a ballroom," Keith recalls. "It was a huge dance club. And it was empty that night." For Keith, however, Hendrix filled the venue with his gigantic talent: "I was absolutely magnetically mesmerized." Her mesmerized state was not that of a novice in these matters: "I had loved the blues long before the Stones even existed. In fact, part of my attraction to Keith was based on our love for the blues. Partly why Jimi trusted me was because of my commitment to the music." Asked whether Hendrix was the best guitarist she'd ever heard, she says, "I think 'best' is the wrong word to use. I would have felt that he was the most innovative." She had certainly never seen someone whose playing was a matter not so much of labor but of symbiosis: "He was so completely involved with the guitar. In those days, he couldn't do anything wrong with the guitar, because it was so much a part of him."

Keith befriended the guitarist that night. She got the impression that the belief in his talent that she communicated to him was profoundly appreciated. Though Keith says she never saw any bitterness from Hendrix about his "undiscovered" status, he was certainly acutely conscious of it: "I think there was frustration and a sort of sadness, because he knew how unique he was with the guitar." Hendrix, though, kept his sadness to himself: "He just accepted that it was a personal thing and it wasn't to be acknowledged amongst the masses."

As she got to know him, Keith realized it wasn't only his talent that made Hendrix different. Her new friend was a huge fan of Bob Dylan: "He thought that Bob Dylan was a genius." Many people did, of course, but in an age of few "crossovers" not many of those people were black. Keith is of the opinion that Hendrix's disregard for what people of his race were supposed to have tastes for was wrapped up in a general refusal to conform to others' musical expectations: "He, like a lot of his peers, wanted to break out of the restrictions that being black was giving to black performers."

Keith remembers Hendrix playing his instrument incessantly during this time frame: "Every time he sat down, he would play the guitar. The moment he stopped doing something, he would pick up a guitar and play it—sometimes sort of unconsciously, and he would talk at the same time." She adds, "You never got the feeling that he was 'practicing.' Practicing, to me, seems like one trying to improve a technique, and I don't think Hendrix ever felt the need to improve on anything in that way."

Keith and Hendrix spent a lot of time at the apartment of two friends of hers, Roberta Goldstein and Mark Hoffman (not Kauffman, as has been erroneously reported). The apartment's décor was almost exclusively red. It was only when a journalist pointed out to Keith that, in his performance of his song "Red House" at the 1970 Isle of Wight Festival, Hendrix sang "'Cos my Linda doesn't live here any more" that it occurred to her that this apartment might have been instrumental in the song's origin: "We did refer to it as the Red House or the Red Place or the Red Apartment or whatever." Keith remembers that Hendrix had the song partly written at this stage: " 'Red House' is very much a standard blues song, and he had been kind of messing around with it. It was in progress when I met him. It was something he just played acoustically or he just played around the house. Then he developed it into that."

That Hendrix could write if he chose—and not just semi-generic blues numbers—was something Keith took as a given, despite his lack of productivity in that area thus far: "I felt that was just a function, really, of his environment. I thought that, given the proper scheduling and so on, it was obvious that he would be able to write songs. He was never left alone enough to do it." Asked if Hendrix shared her confidence in him, Keith replies, "For writing songs, yes. Not for singing."

Keith told Hendrix he was too talented for Knight, which was patently true, but it was only when Keith lent him a white Fender Stratocaster that Hendrix plucked up sufficient courage to leave the Squires. The guitar, in fact, belonged to Keith Richards, but Hendrix never returned it. By mid-1966, Hendrix had finally taken the plunge and formed a group in which nobody would be able to tell him that he was too wild, too pretty, or too anything else. Jimmy James and the Blue Flames was built around the creative nucleus of Hendrix and Randy "California" Wolfe, a 15-year-old with a precocious gift for guitar playing, who would later achieve success with Spirit. It would seem that in this period, Hendrix began to dip his toe, very tentatively, into songwriting (though Hendrix did receive a cowriter's credit on the Curtis Knight songs "Hornet's Nest" and "Welcome Home"). One of the songs in the Blue Flames' repertoire was a Hendrix original called "Mr. Bad Luck," later to become "Look Over Yonder." Friend Billy Kulik recalls that during this period Hendrix had composed a primitive version of "3rd Stone from the Sun." "Takin' Care of No Business"—which became an outtake from *Axis: Bold As Love*—also dates from the Greenwich Village days. In addition, Diane Carpenter (also known as Regina), a girlfriend of Hendrix's who would, in 1966, allegedly give birth to Hendrix's illegitimate daughter, has recalled that he had already written part of "The Wind Cries Mary" for her as a fragment of poetry, and claimed that "Long Hot Summer Night"—later to turn up on *Electric Ladyland*—was also written before his departure to Britain.

Hendrix would seem to have been working his way toward writing other songs. Another Village musician, Ken Pine, has said that when he heard *Are You Experienced* he recalled riffs and melodies on it being played by Hendrix in New York. Linda Keith's recollection is similar: "All the ones on *Are You Experienced*, I'd heard in their baby stages. I might be wrong, but I was not surprised by any song on the album." She adds of those baby-stage compositions, "I think they were more than snatches. I think some of them were developed songs."

Keith was so convinced of Hendrix's talents that she arranged for important music business people to see him in action in New York. The first, and obvious, person was Andrew Loog Oldham, the manager of her boyfriend's band. "Somehow or other Jimi got a week at the Cafe Au Go Go— or two weeks, even—and I took Andrew down there and I was astonished that Andrew wasn't interested," she says. "In those days, Jimi didn't really give bad performances. He just did his thing and he was absolutely amazing."

"I missed Jimi Hendrix for some very sound reasons," says Oldham. "You act on instinct. I wasn't getting on very well with Linda Keith, and she asked me to take her out. We went out to dinner and then she said, 'Come along to this club.'

My mind was going, 'What am I doing here? I'm out in a club with the girlfriend of my guitarist and the best friend of my wife and I don't like it.' There was something in the air that had her introducing Hendrix to me across the room and not in person. Kind of, 'See him, Andrew, but you can't meet him.' Very strange. Hendrix didn't seem to be talking to her that night, although there was an intimate but hostile undercurrent of familiarity in the room between them." Oldham says he remembers virtually nothing about Hendrix's performance that night: "Quite honestly, you could have put Bob Dylan, anybody, in front of me. I wasn't concentrating. Then, when it became apparent that she had inclinations towards Jimi Hendrix, I just felt uncomfortable." He adds, "I didn't know she was offering me the act. And if I've got that wrong then that's two people's versions of the truth. She might have said it and I didn't hear her." However, he does admit, "If I had been all *compos mentis* I still would have missed Jimi Hendrix. The way that I served artists, I don't think I could have contributed anything towards Jimi Hendrix. I didn't fall in love with him and that was what it takes for me to work with people. He didn't pull me away from the domestic malaise I was dealing with in my head." He also adds a practicality-related drawback: "My day job was the Rolling Stones. In terms of making somebody into a star, I couldn't have done that because of my agenda with the Rolling Stones." Oldham is able to recognize Hendrix's abilities now: "The man was an incredible talent. If you add up all the people who still have an incredible cause and effect on people, [it's] Bob Dylan, Jimi Hendrix, and Jim Morrison. If I had to, I redeemed myself when Lou Adler and John Philips turned 'round and said, 'Which English acts do we need for the Monterey Pop Festival?' I said, 'That's easy: the Who and Jimi Hendrix.'"

Sire Records' cofounder Seymour Stein was the next record industry figure Keith invited to see Hendrix play. Stein and his partner, Richard Gottehrer, saw Hendrix perform at another New York venue. Keith says of the pair's reaction, "It was a kind of shoulder shrug: 'Nah, nah, I don't think so. Not my sort of thing.'"

Yet Stein has different memories: "Linda Keith has a great ear and [later] turned me on to Arthur Brown, but in the end he signed with another label. She told me about this guy Jimmy James: 'He's fabulous, blah blah blah.' This was maybe a couple of months after I had started Sire Records. She has very good taste so I will go with her." Stein and Gottehrer were impressed by what they saw, including the fact that Hendrix seemed to have some songs of his own. "The first thing I look for is original songs," says Stein. "A number of songs that he played that night—whether he had written them or not—were not songs that I had heard before." However, the partners did not manage to get backstage to meet Hendrix. "At the end of the gig, he pulled a Who and started breaking up the guitar," says Stein. "He broke this guitar, but it was *her* guitar. She became hysterical, so I never got to meet him. You would have thought that she had witnessed her best friend being murdered in front of her."

The Sire partners arranged to catch another New York Hendrix show. "We wanted to go back and meet him," says Stein. "The club was on Eighth Street." However, it seemed that the pair were destined never to hook up with Hendrix.

"We saw him a second time and the same thing happened. We wanted to see him again, and then she got into another fight with him." Stein says that, as long as Hendrix was not expecting a big advance, he would have signed him. "I thought that he was an amazing guitar player. All of the little tricks that he had—playing the guitar with his teeth and everything like that. . . . Beyond that, he was a great musician. I really liked very much what I heard and what I saw. In all fairness, I wish I had the opportunity. If I could've, I would've. I think she's forgetting the fact that I saw him under the worst possible conditions. I've fucked up over the years, but this wasn't one of the occasions, I can assure you. I thought he was brilliant."

The third connection Keith tried to forge between Hendrix and an industry figure was the one that "took." In the first week of July 1966, the British band the Animals were due to play a gig in Central Park on what was their unofficial farewell tour. Chas Chandler, the Animals' towering and opinionated bassist, had his sights set on a production career. Upon running into him, Keith, who had never spoken to Chandler before, suggested she knew a person who might be the ideal act with which to start that new career. Chandler caught a Blue Flames show and was instantly smitten. "I think he was mindblown," says Keith. Chandler returned to New York as soon as the Animals' tour was over and took Hendrix back to his home country.

"Jimi wasn't known at all at this time, but I hadn't any doubt in my mind," Chandler was later to say of his discovery of Hendrix. "To me, he was fantastic. I thought there must be a catch somewhere. Why hadn't anyone else discovered him?" The truth was, there was no catch. Hendrix—awesome talent though he was—had fallen through the net due to a mixture of incredible bad luck and crossed wires. He made up for his long wait for discovery in spades, though: merely months later, he was revolutionizing popular music—and the electric guitar—with "Purple Haze."

Lonnie Youngblood offers a couple of additional reasons for Hendrix's undiscovered status. "Well, first of all, you got to remember he was a wanderer. Jimmy traveled light. Jimmy traveled with his guitar in a bag and clothes in another bag. Jimmy wouldn't stay around. Another thing: Jimmy played with a lot of people, but I think Jimmy was more of the problem, 'cos there was something else Jimmy wanted. It wasn't the people who didn't recognize how great Jimmy was. Jimmy didn't want to be locked in. Jimmy at that time had another agenda. Jimmy didn't want to be locked in with *nobody*, because there was something he wanted doing. That was the bottom line." For Youngblood, Hendrix's wandering spirit paid off with the strange and wonderful new sounds he was to start making upon his arrival in Britain. "There was something inside of him that was raving to come out, and it finally came out."

arriving in London

ON SEPTEMBER 23, 1966, Jimi Hendrix, his new manager Chas Chandler, and Animals roadie Terry McVay flew from JFK airport to London's Heathrow airport. It is presumed that during the flight, the decision was made to change the spelling of Hendrix's first name to Jimi, and to revert to his real surname.

On arrival the following morning, Chandler decided to take Hendrix to the flat of keyboardist Zoot Money, the zany and much-loved leader of the Big Roll Band, an ensemble that was highly successful on the U.K. live circuit. Hendrix jammed a little on the instruments lying around Money's flat. In the flat upstairs resided Kathy Etchingham and Angela King, archetypal sixties London "birds" who lived for pleasure in a city in which—seething as it was with hedonistic pop music talent—there was plenty to be had. Etchingham, a hairdresser, knew Chandler and was friendly with several pop stars including Keith Moon and Brian Jones. Money's wife Ronnie came up to tell Etchingham that Chandler had brought in someone who looked like the Wild Man of Borneo. "I was in bed so I didn't get up so I didn't meet him," remembers Etchingham.

Etchingham didn't have to wait long, however, until her path crossed Hendrix's. "We went down to the Scotch later that night and Chas was down there with him," she says. "The Scotch" was the Scotch of St. James, one of several clubs in London catering to the new rock aristocracy that had emerged in London since the Beatles had kicked off the beat revolution. Venues where people involved in the pop industry and their friends could mingle without being bothered by autograph hunters and the like, they included the Speakeasy, Blaises, and the Bag O' Nails. The Scotch was probably the most prestigious in terms of famous clientele, and it was probably for this reason that Chandler decided to showcase his new talent there by arranging for Hendrix to perform on the club's stage that evening. "He was performing when I arrived," Etchingham recalls. "Just playing. I think he only did one or two [songs] because he didn't have a work permit, so he wasn't allowed to work, with or without pay, so Chas wouldn't let him stay on for very long in case the immigration were watching." Etchingham recalls some well-known faces in the crowd: "Georgie Fame was there. Zoot Money was there. I don't know if [Eric Burdon] was there or not, but he certainly came 'round to the hotel later that evening." Etchingham reveals that she spoke to Hendrix almost immediately. Hendrix joined her at the table she was sharing with, among others, Linda Keith and Ronnie Money: "Soon as he came off stage, soon as I sat down. Within minutes. Linda went upstairs to the loo and I think he just said, 'Can I just speak to you for a moment?' and I moved over. I thought he was very nice. Unusual. Interesting. Reasonably impressed, I suppose."

When a violent fracas occurred at the table, a panic-stricken Chandler—nervous about anything that could get Hendrix deported—asked Etchingham to take Hendrix back to Hyde Park Towers, the rather shabby Bayswater hotel he had booked him into. To find the way by himself would have been beyond Hendrix, a newcomer to London. Etchingham stayed with Hendrix that night. They were to remain a couple for most of the rest of Hendrix's life.

Within the first couple of days of his arrival in London, Hendrix, with Etchingham beside him, decided to call his father to let him know of the exciting new development in his career. Says Etchingham, "I got the impression that his relationship wasn't that close. He couldn't wait to phone his dad up and say, 'Look, I'm over in England, see? So there.' Because his dad had always told him that he'd never be anything, and to get a job as a laborer, and put him down and sort of said, 'You'll never be any good.'" The call did not go the way Hendrix was clearly imagining it would. Not having a penny to his name, he called collect. Hendrix senior did not believe at first that his son was halfway around the world, but when Jimi passed the phone to Etchingham and he heard her distinctively English tones he was convinced—and hung up, furious that he was paying for an international call. Hendrix was dismayed.

In contrast to the indifference often shown Hendrix in his native land, just about everybody on the music scene in London who witnessed Hendrix performing during his first couple of months there was immediately excited by him. Two such instant converts were Chris Stamp and Kit Lambert, who, as managers of the Who, knew something about great music and incendiary virtuosity. It's difficult to pinpoint exactly when the pair first clapped eyes on Hendrix. Though many reference books cite September 27, 1966, when Hendrix was jamming with a group called the VIPs at the Scotch of St. James, Stamp is fairly sure the performance he saw was at the Bag O' Nails, thus calling the date into question. What is not in question, however, is that this sighting would be hugely important in Hendrix's life.

"He just got up and jammed with the band who were playing," Stamp recollects. "I've no idea who they were to this day."
He is certain, however, that it wasn't one of the jam sessions
that celebrated keyboardist Brian Auger arranged with Jimi: "I
don't think even Jimi would have totally obliterated me to the
fact that Brian Auger was playing." Stamp found his attention
diverted from his socializing by Hendrix's technique. "It wasn't
the sort of place we went and sat and looked at the group. He
got up and started to play on his guitar. It was suddenly very
different in some way to make me look. I looked and I saw this
guy and I noticed he looked quite sort of extraordinary. So it
was a visual thing. Then I noticed he was playing left hand."
On top of the arresting guitar style and the charisma was a
striking musicality. "He was just making that connection
between things that are called blues or soul. They just impact
you on a different level. . . . I was totally drawn in, totally fascinated by this being. It was just an extraordinary moment."
Not that even a seasoned guider of talent like Stamp knew
quite what he had before him: "There was also the complica-
tion. . . . He wasn't a star of an obvious nature. Eric Clapton
was this great guitarist who was also a really good-looking guy.
The same with Jeff Beck. One couldn't define Jimi. If you were
to say, 'Is this guy a star?,' looking at him, you would think he
was very fascinating, but you wouldn't necessarily think he was
a star. It wasn't on that basis. We were attracted to working on
him for a mix of reasons. I can't say for Kit, [but] I was fascinated by his guitar playing. I was fascinated by the general sort
of feel, the look of this guy. All of it sort of worked." They
made a beeline for the newcomer: "Kit and I then went up to
say, 'Hi.' Chas was there and we knew Chas."

The obvious ways for the pair to become involved, how-ever, were closed off to them: "When we talked to Chas, Chas said him and Mike Jeffries [sic] were partners, so they were gonna be doing the management. And then Chas said he was gonna be doing the producing. . . ." There was, though, one other possibility. Stamp and Lambert were toy-ing with an idea that would eventually manifest itself as Track Records. "We said we'd love to talk, because we were think-ing of forming a label. It wasn't sort of like a serious business discussion down there at the Bag O' Nails, but it showed interest. So Chas was very keen to get together with Kit and I again and talk about it with Mike Jeffries [sic]."

Before Hendrix's camp could even think about such mat-ters, however, there was the not inconsiderable matter of obtaining residence and work permits for Britain, neither of which Hendrix had. Chandler had only managed to effect Hendrix's entry into the country by persuading New York songwriter Scott English—cowriter of Animals hit "It's My Life"—to swear a false statement that he had known Hendrix for several years, and then by engaging in heated debate with officials at Heathrow Airport and claiming that Hendrix was a songwriter who was visiting the country to collect royal-ties. "He couldn't work here until he had a permit," points out Etchingham. "That was the number one priority." The mak-ing and marketing of Hendrix would have proved impossible without that vital document, starting with the trip to France at which the Jimi Hendrix Experience made its debut. "He couldn't have gone to France because he wouldn't have been able to come back in again, 'cos in those days you had to have a visa to come here from France," says Etchingham. "So he couldn't do anything. He couldn't work abroad or anything."

The necessary permits were obtained with astonishing speed and in circumstances shrouded in mystery by Mike Jeffery, manager of the Animals and the man who would be comanager of Jimi Hendrix. (Jeffery, incidentally, is often referred to as "Jeffries" by those quoted in this text: most people who knew him got his name slightly wrong, for some reason.) As to how Jeffery managed to swing these crucial pieces of paperwork, Etchingham says, "Well, we don't know. He just turned up at the hotel with it one day and said, 'Right, OK, let's order a round of drinks, there's your visa.' And he had a work permit. Chas couldn't have done that without Mike Jeffries [sic]." Etchingham adds, "He had to bring Mike Jeffries in because he didn't have the money or the contacts that he needed to be able to get Jimi off the ground by himself."

This was presumably the only reason that Chandler was prepared to work with someone who had quite obviously swindled him out of millions: after having played on records with the Animals that had shifted huge amounts of money, Chandler had almost nothing to show for it. As well as the contacts and finances Etchingham mentions, Noel Redding—who would shortly be recruited as bass player for the Jimi Hendrix Experience—claims one other reason that made it necessary for Chandler to allow Jeffery to become part of the management team: "He was still signed to him through the Animals. I only sussed [that] about twenty years ago." For Redding, it was obvious from the get-go that Jeffery was not motivated by art. "Jeffries [sic] was basically in the background. He was the guy who was just stealing all the money." He does add, however, "I always got on well with Jeffries personally, for some funny reason."

Such matters were well into the future, however. What was occupying the Hendrix camp in those early days in London was the need to surround Hendrix with a group of musicians who could best project his talent. It would seem that the first thing to occur to Chandler was not to audition musicians, but to graft Hendrix onto an already existing ensemble. The ensemble he chose was the Brian Auger Trinity, a blues/jazz group who until recently had been a part of the talent-oozing Steampacket aggregation, through whose ranks Rod Stewart and Long John Baldry had passed.

Auger, the band's keyboardist and leader, recalls the approach from Chandler: "He called me. He said, 'Please come up to the office.' This sounded fairly serious, when somebody asked you to come to their management office for something. So I jumped into the tube and went down to Gerrard Street, where they had their office, and I spoke to him and Mike Jeffery. Chas said, 'I've got this unbelievable guitar player.' I said, 'Fine.' 'And I think that he should front your band'—I think were his exact words. I said, 'Well, that's fantastic, Chas, but I have a guitar player [Vic Briggs], and also, Julie Driscoll fronts my band.' He said, 'Yeah, but this guy is just unbelievable. I think your band will be ideal for him to be out there.'"

Though the suggestion of such a mercenary dismissal of his current colleagues might have taken Auger aback, he wasn't overly surprised that Chandler should have chosen his group as the one in which to set Hendrix's brilliance. "There weren't too many organ players who had come off the jazz scene and could play just about anything the same way that I could, and could cut it on jazz terms, blues terms, whichever, and that were interested in that side of the business." Nevertheless, the deal Chandler proposed was out of the question. Instead, Auger came up with a proposition for Chandler: "'If this guy is so good, then we're playing at the Cromwellian on Friday and we're playing at the Bag O' Nails and some other clubs in London. Why don't you bring the guy down and he can sit in with my band and you can show him around the scene in London? This isn't gonna cost you anything and we'll get an idea of what this guy is all about.'"

Chandler took Auger up on this offer, but this left him with the prospect of creating a band for Hendrix the hard, traditional way: by arranging auditions and going through the tedious process of listening to the efforts of young hopefuls. He was saved from such tedium, however, by the happy coincidence that at that point in time, his old friend and Animals colleague Eric Burdon was arranging auditions for a new permutation of that band. The new Animals—or Eric Burdon & the Animals, as they were to be formally known— would be a group in tune with the psychedelic music Burdon had recently witnessed firsthand in San Francisco. The auditions were being held at yet another London club, Birdland. One young hopeful who turned up looking for a path to instant fame and riches was Noel Redding.

Redding was born on Christmas Day, 1945, in Folkestone, Kent. He was a lead guitarist whose first band had been called the Burnettes. "We worked away and we became very popular down in Kent," he recalls. "[We] went to Germany when I was 18. I worked in Germany with the Burnettes 'til

'65." The Burnettes were renamed the Loving Kind and acquired not only a good manager—Gordon Mills, who would steer the likes of Engelbert Humperdinck and Tom Jones to stardom—but recording work. "We did three singles for Pye-Piccadilly. And we did actual demo sessions for Gerry Dorsey—Humperdinck." Redding decided to quit the band in the summer of 1966, however, when Mills sent them on a 10-hour trip to Cardiff, Wales, in the mistaken belief that he'd booked them in for a gig (it was actually the following week). Redding wryly recalls Mills's reaction to his resignation. "Gordon Mills phoned me up and said, 'You'll never work again.'"

Redding's audition for the Animals was not completely on a whim: "I went down there because Eric Burdon, about six months previously—we were playing up in London in a club—he come up and sung a couple of songs with us, and he said he was well impressed with the band. I played with Eric and he vaguely remembered me." Though Redding failed to get the Animals gig, the legend that it had already been given to Vic Briggs is inaccurate: Briggs didn't get the job until that October—and in fact was offered it when he was playing in France for Johnny Halliday, whose support act was the Jimi Hendrix Experience, which Redding had by then been a member of for nearly three weeks. It should also be pointed out that the first, brief incarnation of the new Animals featured one Tom Parker on keyboards (he was employed for a single U.K. tour) rather than a second guitarist. Whatever the reason for Burdon declining Redding's services, it was certainly a lucky break for Redding. Chandler and Hendrix, along with Etchingham, had been observing the proceedings at Birdland, looking for their own recruits. "That's when Chas came up and said can I play bass," recalls Redding. "I said, 'No, but I'll give it a go.' I was handed this bass, which was Chas's bass."

An impromptu audition for Hendrix's prospective new band then took place, literally in the same room. "We went through three tunes with no vocals," Redding says. "As far as I can recall it was 'Have Mercy,' 'Land of 1,000 Dances,' and Hendrix told me the chords for 'Hey Joe.' We just played it through. The drummer was Aynsley Dunbar. Keyboard player was [Mike] O'Neill, who used to have that band Nero and the Gladiators." Of Hendrix's guitar playing that day, Redding says, "The first play we had, he wasn't really playing lead. He was just playing rhythm, basically. I think he was trying to suss out people." Asked whether, as a fellow guitarist, he appreciated the extent of the talent of the man with whom he was jamming, Redding replies, "It was very early, but my mum always said that I came home on the train and said, 'This bloke's really good.'" He adds, however, "It wasn't until when we did our first tour in France with Johnny Halliday that I sussed out the guy was *really* good." Redding's first impressions of Hendrix as a person were superficial ones. "I'd met Americans before when I'd worked in Germany, so I always had this thing: I sort of liked Americans, for some funny reason. Two other impressions was, he was wearing this horrible raincoat and it wasn't raining, and he had winklepickers on, by which time winklepickers had gone out of vogue: everyone was wearing those Cuban-heel things."

Though this was the first time Redding had attempted to seriously play the instrument in his hands, he seemed to create a good impression. "This American gentleman said, 'Can I have a chat with you?'" recalls Redding of Hendrix. "So we went to this little pub next door and we sat in the corner. . . . I found the guy highly polite and really nice." Inevitably, the two musicians discussed music. "He asked me all about the English music situation at that point, which was Kinks, Small Faces, the Move, et cetera, et cetera. I'd never been to America so I asked him had he ever seen Sam Cooke, had he ever seen Booker T, that sort of stuff. We had a pint of best bitter each and he said would I join his group. And that was it." Redding is convinced that it is this personal connection as much as anything that got him the job: "He'd never been in England and I think he sort of appreciated the fact that we just went down the pub and talked about the music." This just left the formalities to be arranged: "After I came back two days later and met up with Jeffries [sic], he said, 'You have to move to London.'"

Etchingham says, "Noel's memory is different from mine. I don't remember going 'round to the pub at all and having a pint. And Jimi didn't drink pints. So I think that's just Noel thinking everybody has a pint. If I remember rightly, we left with Chas and [Chandler's girlfriend] Lotta and he'd already gone. I don't think we went into any pub 'cos if we had've done, I'd have remembered standing there talking to him, but I didn't actually meet him again until later." As to the reasoning behind Redding's lightning-fast appointment, she says, "I can remember Chas saying, 'Look, he can play a solid bass line so, fine. He looks all right, so he looks fine.' They didn't want anybody that was going to do anything fancy. They didn't want anybody trying to do their own thing on stage."

It was possibly on the same evening as Redding's audition that Hendrix took up Auger's offer to sit in with his band.

This can't be said with certainty, however, because of differences in the recollections of those present as to the location. Most sources cite Blaises as the venue. Auger himself says it was the Cromwellian. Vic Briggs, the man in Auger's band nudged aside to make room for Hendrix for the jam, swears it was the Scotch of St. James. This author, having been impressed by Briggs's memory when interviewing him for a book on the Animals, is inclined to go with Briggs. Whatever the venue, this would be one of several jams that would help Hendrix's name become a buzzword in musical circles in his first few weeks in England's capital. Such jams were a fixture of the U.K. music scene at the time—though they did not usually catapult people to such instant cult status.

"The one thing that sticks in my mind more than anything else," recalls Vic Briggs, "is that when I walked into the Scotch of St. James on the night, this waiter came up to me and said, 'You should have seen the wild man that Chas Chandler had down here last night.' My guess would be that it was the 28th. September 27th was a Tuesday, and the gig was on a Wednesday or a Thursday." Briggs recalls Chandler arriving as the Trinity was setting up: "It was unusual. Nobody came to the Scotch at 9:30 at night. He said to me, 'Look, this guy is new in London and he's really good and we'd like him to sit in. Is it okay to use your amp?' He introduced me to Jimi." Briggs liked the newcomer. "He was pleasant, he was friendly, he was certainly polite—and humble. . . . I said, 'Here's my amp and you're welcome to use it. Do you need a guitar?' And he goes, 'No, man. I got my own. I play left-handed.'"

Briggs was slightly surprised to see that the newcomer's guitar was the same make as his own: a Fender Stratocaster

"That wasn't an 'in' guitar at that time," he recalls. "They were slightly unfashionable. I think Jeff Beck, Clapton, Peter Green—they all played Les Pauls. Strats were out because Strats were like Hank Marvin—he wasn't blues. Hank was an excellent guitar player, but you know how it is in England: Hank Marvin was really hot, then all of a sudden there's the Beatles and this movement away from the more kind of strait-laced pop of Cliff Richard and the Shadows, so the Shadows immediately become like family [entertainment]." Briggs was also surprised that Hendrix's guitar was actually a right-handed model, which he played upside down with the strings transposed. "I asked him about that," says Briggs. "I knew there was left-handed Strats available. I said, 'How come you don't play a left-handed Strat?' He said, 'They're shit, man. They're very badly made.'"

Briggs owned a Marshall stack, and this particular evening may well have been Hendrix's first exposure to that make of amplifiers he would be most closely associated with. (Briggs's setup was actually an experimental one, of which there were only a few made, with twelve six-inch speakers.) "The Scotch was a tiny little room, really tiny, and he walked up to this Marshall stack and he just turned everything way up," says Briggs. "Up to eleven, kind of thing. He must have seen the look on my face because he said to me, 'Don't worry, man—I turn it down on the guitar.' And he did. He wasn't overbearingly loud or anything like that."

Auger takes up the story: "Jimi seemed like a really nice guy, a real sweet man. I said, 'Well what would you like to play, Jim?' He said, 'Can I show you these chords?' and he showed me this sequence of chords, which turned out to be

'Hey Joe.' He said, 'Could you play that?' He gave us the tempo and we started to play." Auger says those in the venue realized just how talented this newcomer was fairly instantaneously: "I think most of the guitar players in the room, their heads turned and they went, 'Oh my God, who is this?' It was pretty amazing, man. It was obvious that this was something else. I think what impressed me most about him was this: I've played with Clapton and Jeff Beck, Jimmy Page, and generally you could spot their roots, which was generally things like B. B. King, Albert King, Freddie King, and on and on. As far as Jimi was concerned, I'd never heard anything like that. It was a unique style of playing. It was blues based, but it had all sorts of other things in it. I just recognized it as being something that was of its own."

Though Auger was overwhelmed by Hendrix's talent, there was still no question of him making space in his group for him. From the point of view of Briggs—who, incidentally, was not told of the approach by Chandler—it would not have been successful anyway. "Brian is very headstrong; he likes to be in charge. At that time, the Steampacket was over and I don't think Brian wanted to have any more headliners over himself, like Long John Baldry. I don't think it would have worked out. Brian wanted to be known for himself as a household name." Briggs himself was not as bowled over by Hendrix as his colleague. "I was not overimpressed," he says. "I thought he was good. He did this whole thing of playing behind the head and playing with his teeth and all that kind of stuff. (By the way, I don't believe he played with his teeth. I believe it was grandstanding. I think he put it to his mouth and then he hammered the strings with his fingers.) I was a bit of a purist and it didn't excite me. I already had quite a technique on the guitar and, to put it succinctly, Jimi didn't do anything that I didn't think that I could do. It's just that it wasn't what I chose to do. I was very jazz-oriented, so I wasn't really into the distortion and the overdrive. That was my first impression."

If Briggs wasn't overwhelmed by Hendrix as a player, he was certainly impressed by him as a person. The two became good friends, something assisted by the fact that when Briggs joined the new Animals not long afterward he fell under the same management umbrella. "He always said to me he loved my guitar playing," recalls Briggs. "Many, many times he said that to me, and I was naturally flattered." He was even more flattered when, in a profile published in *Jackie* magazine in spring 1967, Hendrix listed among "Things I Like," "The guitar playing of Eric Clapton, Jeff Beck, and Vic Briggs."

From that point on, Jimi Hendrix became a regular fixture in London clubs. "Not necessarily jamming all the time, but Chas would always have him in a club somewhere," explains Briggs. "Usually the Scotch. The Scotch was the happening club at that time." It was an astute move: the presentation of this new talent to the cognoscenti created an unstoppable word of mouth that would make Hendrix a living legend within the blink of a music industry eye.

forming the Experience

ON OCTOBER 1, 1966, Cream was playing a gig at Regent Polytechnic in London. Although the band had yet to release a record, they were already something of a talking point. A supergroup before that term was invented, Cream matched former Yardbirds and Bluesbreakers virtuoso guitarist Eric Clapton with the turbocharged ex-rhythm section of the Graham Bond Organization—bassist Jack Bruce and drummer Ginger Baker. Thus the men whom many people considered the three best musicians in London were playing together. This was not lost on the band itself: their name was inspired by the perception that they were the crème de la crème.

According to Chas Chandler, Clapton and Bruce had been intrigued after bumping into Chandler a couple of days before this gig and hearing about his new discovery. Chandler told them it wouldn't be fair if he took up the offer they made for Hendrix to jam with them: "You're mates of mine. You can't let me do this to you." This remark apparently further interested the two. Chandler, frankly, seems to have been prone to myth making, and one should take this story with a pinch of salt. When Hendrix did jam with the band on the evening in question, however, the results seem to have been the stuff of which myths are made.

"Chas went up to the stage and Eric leaned down and he said, 'I've got this guy with me from America,'" recalls Etchingham of the show. "I was standing quite a way back with Jimi and Lotta. And then there was some talk amongst them. Ginger Baker [or] Jack Bruce, one of them, shook his head. And then he came back and some more was said. [Clapton] played a bit more and then he said, 'We're going to introduce a guy that's turned up from America, Jimi Hendrix.' He tried to hand Jimi his guitar and I was behind him with his own guitar in a case. Jimi took the case off me and opened it on the stage. There was a bit of fiddling around while they plugged it in." Cream, and Clapton especially, had no idea what was about to hit them. "We were giggling, because we knew he was really good," says Etchingham. "[Clapton] walked to the side of the stage and lit a ciggie."

Hendrix proceeded to perform a showstopping version of "Killing Floor," a song that, coincidentally, Clapton had always found beyond even his advanced abilities. Clapton later related that Hendrix "stole the show." Chandler's assertion that he found a stunned Clapton backstage, trying to put a match to a cigarette with shaking fingers, was almost certainly another Chandler tall tale, but Etchingham says, "I don't think he was shaking at all, but he did say, 'Bloody hell, he's good.'" Suddenly there was a new order. If he didn't realize it that particular night, there is little doubt that during this period Clapton apprehended that the elevated status that had led to the scrawling of "CLAPTON IS GOD" graffiti on London walls had been instantly undermined by the arrival of a new, superior deity.

Not that Hendrix would necessarily have agreed with the perception of the hierarchy prior to his arrival on the scene. Etchingham claims, "From a technical point of view, he preferred Jeff Beck's work."

Meanwhile, Hendrix and his managers were trying to find a drummer for the group. In addition to Dunbar, two others were auditioned. "There was another guy who we played with, a guy from up north somewhere," says Redding. "I can't remember the guy's name." The other auditionee was John "Mitch" Mitchell. Mitchell had just been fired, along with the rest of his colleagues, from Georgie Fame's backing group (ironically titled, like Hendrix's previous group, the Blue Flames). "By which time Jimi and Chas were asking *me*," recalls Redding. "So I said, 'Well I prefer a straight drummer.' And Jimi said, 'Yes,' Chas, 'I dunno' or whatever." Such indecision and conflicting stances possibly made what happened next inevitable: "He only got the job because of the toss of a coin," says Etchingham of Mitchell. "I was there when he was auditioned and Aynsley Dunbar was auditioned and they tossed a coin in the back of a cab and it came down for Mitch. Jimi didn't care between the two of them and both drummers were okay with him."

Bizarre and arbitrary as this recruitment method may have been, it was necessitated by the move to act quickly. French pop idol Johnny Halliday had been one of the overwhelmed observers at a recent Hendrix club appearance and had offered him a support slot on his forthcoming French tour. Chandler, showing the quick wits and slight deviousness that are probably essential to being a good manager, had accepted the offer despite not having any musicians with whom to back Hendrix.

Mitchell was born on July 9, 1946, in Middlesex, just outside London. He had enjoyed considerable success as a child actor, but by about age 15 he'd decided he wanted to be a drummer. He was taught to play by a tutor called Jim Marshall, who would later become far better known as the manufacturer of Jimi Hendrix's guitar amplifiers of choice. Of

Mitchell, Marshall recalls, "He was my shop boy first of all on a Saturday. Then he asked me to teach him to play the drums." Marshall reports that Mitchell didn't bother agonizing about whether he was going to continue his acting career when he took up the instrument: "He stopped that almost immediately." Mitchell has often been accused of having a cavalier, even selfish attitude in life, and Marshall acknowledges this in revealing—with a laugh—"Well, he was not a 100 percent pupil, but I suppose his acting career made him a bit of a showman." Nevertheless, Mitchell's dilettante attitude toward studying did not prevent him from taking on board his tutor's skills, and by the time he auditioned with Hendrix he had developed into a striking musician. "All my pupils had to learn everything: jazz, big bands, the lot, and he had that sort of feel of jazz and big band, plus his bit of showmanship and I suppose that impressed Jimi Hendrix. I think it suited Jimi Hendrix's style."

Mitchell's eventual graduation to the Blue Flames (by way, incidentally, of a brief stint in a group with Vic Briggs called Peter Nelson and the Travellers) denoted his advanced abilities: pianist Fame was one of the most highly regarded musicians in Britain at the time. Yet Hendrix friend and biographer Chris Welch recalls that Mitchell blossomed rapidly within the Experience. "I already knew Mitch from Georgie Fame and the Blue Flames. Then when he appeared with Jimi, I think Jimi inspired him so much. He gave him so much freedom that he just exploded. Everybody was saying, 'Wow, is that Mitch playing the drums?' It seemed like a revelation." Redding adds, "He was jazzy and very flamboyant. I think he was similar to [Keith] Moon. Moon was a brilliant drummer." In an era of extraordinary drum talent that included not only Moon but Ginger Baker, Redding has no doubts about who was the top dog: "I'd say Mitchell was probably the best at the time."

On Thursday, October 6, 1966, the finalized lineup of the Jimi Hendrix Experience—destined to be one of the greatest ensembles in the history of popular music—rehearsed for the very first time. This debut was probably at Aberbach Publishing House in London, a venue that would be the setting for most of the Experience's few rehearsals. The room, in Savile Row, was owned by the Shadows, which had been Britain's top group before the Beatles hit the scene. "They'd turned it into a rehearsal room and a place they could hang out when they were in London," recalls Redding. "We were on the second floor, and it was a small room with a window. Our rehearsals were basically plugging in, no vocal, just running through stuff." This first rehearsal lasted from 1:00 P.M. to 5:30 P.M. and was not particularly different, or better, than subsequent ones. "Jimi refused to sing," says Redding. "We used to basically just play a couple of backing tracks and go down the pub. After that, we didn't have to rehearse, really."

The rehearsal saw Redding having to come to grips not just with new colleagues but with a new instrument. It wasn't as difficult as he had feared. "All I did —in me brain—was to take off the top two strings on the guitar, and then it's an octave down or whatever it is. Then Chandler showed me a good couple of things on the bass, like walking bass, et cetera. I just sort of adapted to it." Though he adapted, he retained a lead guitarist's sensibilities. "I also was playing chords on it, which I think Jimi liked. A lot of songs, like 'Stone Free,' I'm basically playing chords in the chorus."

It was quite unusual at the time for a band not to have a fourth member, either a rhythm guitarist or a keyboardist. Redding and Etchingham have different memories of the rationale for the trio format.

"They kept it down to a trio on purpose so that Jimi would stand out," says Etchingham. "He was so versatile that they felt they didn't need anybody else. There was never any intention to have a fourth member." Redding claims, however, that the three-piece setup was settled upon in a less deliberate manner. "At some point we did consider me playing rhythm, James playing lead, and getting another bass player, which we actually tried once but didn't work. We all decided—well, myself and Hendrix—three-piece and that's it." Redding certainly acknowledges that there was an extraordinary musical alchemy between the three band members. "It worked: Hendrix a blues player, Mitchell a jazz player, and me a rock player. It just worked." Early the following year, Hendrix would express similar sentiments about the rich brew created by the band's varied ingredients to Kevin Swift of *Beat Instrumental* magazine: "If I'd had two bluesmen with me, we would have gone straight into one bag—the blues. That's not for me. This way we can do anything and develop our own music. We might do our own arrangement of a Howlin' Wolf number, followed straight away by 'Wild Thing,' or a Bobby Dylan number. We'll do things our own way and make our own sound."

Of the band's name, incidentally, Redding says, "A lot of people say that Chas thought of it, but actually Michael Jeffries [*sic*] thought of it."

The newly formed Experience was on several counts remarkably similar to the band with whom Hendrix had jammed so memorably at the Regent Polytechnic less than a week before. Like Cream, the Experience was a power trio (though that phrase wasn't in use at the time) with a frenetic, jazz-influenced drummer and a magnetic, dexterous guitarist, playing blues-based, volume-driven music that was always pushing back accepted ideas about song structure and virtuosity. Despite Hendrix's admiration for Clapton, however, all who were on the scene at the time agree that the similarity between the groups seems to have been nothing more than extraordinary coincidence. Nonetheless, it would often be remarked upon in the succeeding months and years—not least by Cream members themselves. Chris Stamp remembers an extraordinary evening spent at Brian Epstein's house following Hendrix's performance at the Saville Theatre at the end of the following January. "Jack Bruce and Eric Clapton and Ginger were there—they were just invited because they were in the audience," he reveals. "They had seen Jimi and all they could talk about was their career was over. He just blew away everything that they thought they were gonna be doing."

For his part, Redding feels that Hendrix may have taken inspiration for the three-piece idea from somewhat more unlikely sources, including the originators of the classic "Shakin' All Over": "Johnny Kidd and the Pirates—that was a three-piece band. I'd played stuff to Jimi by Johnny Kidd. Also, there was another band, from Liverpool, called the Big Three. I was [a fan] of all that lot and I played a lot of stuff to Jim, records. It's the hardest thing to do is play in a three-piece band because every musician has to work their arse off. He'd never heard them before and he'd ask me, 'Who are them guys?'"

One other possible source of inspiration for the Experience's setup is the Who (like the Pirates, technically a three-piece through their non-playing singer), a band of whom Hendrix would have been highly conscious not just because of their fame in Britain but because of his association with them through Stamp. Stamp—although he's unsure whether the Who inspired the setup of the Experience—is convinced that Pete Townshend made a huge impression on Hendrix: "It's quite obvious. We were trying to organize Jimi to do occasional gigs. His entrée was he would be the support band with the Who. He saw Pete Townshend do feedback and break his guitar. Jimi had never seen that before. He took that as his own. Jimi was introduced to Marshall amps because of the Who. There's a lot of cross influence."

When Stamp saw the Experience upon the band's return from France, he was happy with the ensemble Chandler had placed around Hendrix. "I thought that it showcased Jimi. One didn't come away from a Jimi Hendrix Experience gig saying, 'Well what a good *group*.' You come away saying, 'Fuck me—Jimi Hendrix is amazing.' Which is what it was about." Nevertheless, he adds, "I always thought, and still do, that Mitch was a fantastic drummer. There wasn't a drummer that I would rather have had with Jimi other than Keith Moon. In a sense, Mitch Mitchell was vital to Jimi. Really vital. Jimi suddenly had a drummer who could excite him musically."

"Quite happy with it," is Etchingham's memory of Hendrix's feelings about his new band. "They were all pretty spontaneous and didn't have to rehearse too much. They never rehearsed. Very, very seldom. About three times. I think they rehearsed once before they went to Paris and I don't remember any other times. It was that rare." Even when Hendrix became prolific at writing songs, the Experience did not bother, as most bands would, running through them in a rehearsal room before trying to record them in a studio. "We were playing just to satisfy ourselves," says Redding of Experience rehearsals. "We knew we weren't really rehearsing, because we were a lazy load of gits. I'm serious."

This would seem to be the single most astonishing thing about the Jimi Hendrix Experience. Anybody listening to *Are You Experienced* who did not know the background of the album's recording would assume that it was the result of honing songs to perfection in either a rehearsal studio or a live situation. Yet, with the exception of "Hey Joe," not a single song on either the U.S. or U.K. edition of the album had been played by the Experience before the day they recorded it. In light of that fact, the natural, easy flow of the album's tracks and the slickness of their instrumentation seems nothing short of miraculous.

This was testament to the fact that, despite his somewhat arbitrary recruitment methods, Hendrix had stumbled upon a wonderfully cohesive musical unit. It was a unit whose strength came from its members being allowed, within the strictures of the song, to do their own thing. "Basically, very free," Redding says of the remit given to him and Mitchell. "There'd be occasional [Hendrix-dictated] riffs here and there, but then I'd throw in riffs and Mitchell would do stuff. We all worked pretty well together."

Not that the exact format of the band had been decided upon. For instance, the role of singer had yet to be assigned. Today, it seems unthinkable that anybody but Jimi Hendrix could be the lead singer of the Experience, but at this point Hendrix didn't want to fulfill this role. "He didn't think that he could sing, and was very nervous about singing for the first time over here," says Etchingham. Both Redding and Mitchell were sounded out about being the group's vocalist. Hendrix wasn't the only one with insecurities in that department, however: "I was nervous about it as well, because I'd only been a backing singer," says Redding. Meanwhile, the impracticalities of having the man behind the drum set be the group's vocalist were quickly recognized as insurmountable. Etchingham says of Hendrix's vocal shyness: "Chas told him, 'You've got to!' Once he started, he was okay." Though Hendrix reluctantly accepted the necessity of singing, Redding, when asked at what point Hendrix began to gain confidence in his vocals, cites a period several weeks into the future: "After Germany in November '66. We'd been going down well."

Though the new lineup gelled more or less instantly, they felt somewhat frustrated by the technology available to them. Chandler had bought the group some low-power Burns amps. Redding recalls, "We were doing this rehearsal and Hendrix and Mitchell started throwing them against the wall, which completely freaked me out, because I always look after me equipment." The amps' tinniness was the opposite of what Mitchell has described as the "dramatic" sound the group had in mind for themselves. Accordingly, the Experience soon made a visit to the Marshall amplification factory.

Jim Marshall had moved into the manufacture of guitar amplifiers after deciding to open a drum shop in conjunction with his drum school. "I'd taught so many of the top drummers rock and roll that they brought their guitarists in, and the guitarists said to me, 'Why don't you stock amplifiers and guitars?'" Marshall recalls. When he proceeded to do so, young guitarists including Pete Townshend and Ritchie Blackmore told him they found the sound produced by the amplifiers on the market too clean. "A Fender bass sound was the nearest thing to what they wanted, and I realized from that that it was the harmonics of the valve that produced that sort of sound," he explains.

Poaching an 18-year-old wünderkind engineer named Dudley Craven from EMI, Marshall set to work making an amp that would meet the requirements of the young guitarists about town. "He produced six prototypes before I said, 'Ah! That's got to be the Marshall sound,'" says Marshall. "And that's been the Marshall sound ever since." Which is? "Well, most people call it distortion, but really it's the valve harmonics plus a little few things which we do not disclose, obviously. It's overdriven harmonics of the valve."

The Marshall sound was an immediate hit with U.K. guitar players. Vic Briggs remembers of Vox amps: *They weren't loud enough!* At that time, there was no Vox that had more than two 12-inch speakers. Well, Marshall designed a box with four 12-inch speakers. And then they designed two boxes with four 12-inch speakers in each that could be stacked on top of each other. This is eight 12-inch speakers."

Having seen Briggs' Marshall stack—and probably Pete Townshend's—Hendrix decided that he wanted one for himself. The fact that his drummer knew Jim Marshall personally was fortunate. "He said to Mitch, 'I've got to meet this Jim Marshall because I'm Jim Marshall as well'" remembers the amp maker, referring to the fact that the guitarist's full name was James Marshall Hendrix. "So he came along to the shop. This lanky, colored American said to me, 'I'm gonna be the greatest, man.' And I thought, 'Oh crikey—another one wants something for nothing.' But within his next two or three breaths, he said to me, 'I don't want anything given to me. I want to pay the going rate. But what I want is backup wherever I am in the world for repairs, et cetera.'" At first, Marshall had doubts: "I thought, 'Good God—I've only got three countries in the world stocking amplification (that was France, Germany, and Canada). So I thought, 'I'm gonna have a repair man on the road all the time.' But he had a very good roadie, and that roadie spent a couple of weeks at the factory and he was quite bright, so we were never called out once by Jimi. Eventually, Jimi bought four complete setups to place in different parts of the world to save transportation costs—and he paid for all of them."

Of course, Marshall had no way of knowing at this point that Hendrix's ambition to be the "greatest" was actually something that was within his grasp. The first time Marshall heard Hendrix play was a few weeks later at an open-air gig. "Jimi sounded fantastic," recalls Marshall. "He had technique and he had that melodic sound which other guitarists at the time did not: they were playing the three chord trick and all that sort of thing. Heaven knows what he would have grown into if he had not died so young. I don't think he'd reached his peak. It was melodic, well played, and the sound he got was very full." Marshall considers Hendrix to have been his amps' greatest ambassador—despite the occasional bouts of violence directed at them for showmanship purposes, which, according to Marshall, were usually mostly fake anyway. "He was the same as Pete [Townshend], really: he tore quite a lot of the grill fret."

Marshall attributes Hendrix's trademark fat, larger-than-life guitar sound to an understanding of sonics and technology beyond even his highly talented contemporaries: "He was relying purely on the harmonics of the amplifier to produce his sound. He never had the volume of the guitar turned up that much. I think then you would have got too much distortion, whereas he was feeding the amplifier correctly and using the harmonics correctly."

Briggs for one thinks that the impact of the Experience would have been far smaller without the employment of Marshalls: "For the stage sound, they were just absolutely vital. I don't think that he could have done what he done, at least not for maybe a few months or a year, 'til the technology caught up. He couldn't have done it with Voxs. I think that Marshalls was one of those things of being in the right place at the right time."

On October 12, the Experience and Chandler flew to Paris. Their Marshall equipment naturally came with them, but Mitchell had to watch in horror as the new stacks were literally thrown into the cargo hold. The following day, at Novelty, Eveux, the Jimi Hendrix Experience made its first-ever concert appearance. Supporting Long Chris, the Blackbirds, and Johnny Halliday, they played a set, of a mere fifteen minutes in duration, consisting of "Midnight Hour," "Have Mercy," and "Land of 1,000 Dances." It is not known whether "Hey Joe" was performed here. "We went down rather well, which sort of surprised me," says Redding. "We only had three songs. We used to jump on, play, and that was it, but we were on the road so we were excited."

This concert was reviewed, though the anonymous correspondent from *L'Eure Eclair* obviously wasn't aware that this inaugural stage performance by the Experience was history in the making. Of "Halliday's latest discovery," the reviewer said, Hendrix "pulled a wry face on stage . . . and also played the guitar sometimes with his teeth." He summed him up as a "bad mixture of James Brown and Chuck Berry."

On October 14, the same bill played Cinema Rio, Salle Poirel, Nancy. The following day, the acts performed at Salles Des Fates, Villerupt. The biggest show of the tour was to be the final one at the Olympia, Paris, on October 18, where the Brian Auger Trinity was added to the bill. Though not a particularly large venue, it was prestigious and had a discerning clientele. Rehearsals for this gig took place on October 17. Vic Briggs, who was reunited with his old mate Mitch Mitchell at the rehearsal, is convinced that impresario Giorgio Gomelsky had as much to do as Halliday with securing Hendrix this gig: "Giorgio Gomelsky was producing Johnny Halliday records and Giorgio was the producer of the stage show in Paris. Giorgio was a great producer in talent. Even though I don't think he had any [financial] interest in Jimi, I think he saw Jimi's potential."

Brian Auger was aware that this, the Experience's first major gig, would be a baptism of fire: "The Paris audience was very rowdy. If they liked you, they loved you, and if they didn't like you, you might dodge a few tomatoes and things. This show was the first show that I'd seen where the trio was on stage. I stood in the wings. I saw the whole thing." It was a baptism that Hendrix came through with flying colors: "It was pretty incredible, and I realized Jimi was going to be a huge star. Hendrix's playing had advanced. He'd got his own equipment together and he was blazing. He had a great presence on stage and the French just went for it."

Auger's guitarist Vic Briggs was also impressed, despite the distraction of Mike Jeffery having offered him the guitarist's role in the new Animals half an hour before the Trinity was to take the stage. "The show started off with Johnny Halliday's band," he recalls. "They came out and did their thing. The place was jammed. There was mostly men, yelling and screaming and carrying on. Then Jimi came out. They didn't know what to expect, but he just kicked butt. This was early—I think he still hadn't let himself off the leash, so to speak. I do remember he did 'Wild Thing.' I'd always hated 'Wild Thing,' not so much because of the song but because of the Troggs. It was a song that I would never have played in a million years. Jimi played it and I'm going, like, 'Whoa! WHOA! There's really some energy in this. It's really like how the song should be played.'" Briggs was also surprised to see the Experience play Bob Dylan's "Like a Rolling Stone," the last thing he would have expected either a black man or a heavy rocker to perform. "The crowd really loved him," says Briggs. "He pulled out all the stops."

Things did not go so well for the Trinity. "Right after that, we came on," recalls Briggs. "The Brian Auger–Julie Driscoll thing was a jazz oriented blues/rock, and the second that Brian started playing the organ, the audience started booing. They booed through our entire set—three or four songs. Even at the end. In the last song of our set, the Blackbirds came back on, Jimi came back on—a kind of a jam thing. They booed all the way to the end. They wanted heavy rock and roll." That sour finale to the proceedings aside, Redding was understandably elated by the Experience's reception: "It's one of the hardest gigs in the world to do and we did it and went down a storm, so we were all well chuffed."

Amazingly, the Experience's performance was preserved for posterity, and two songs of their set were featured on the 2000 box set *The Jimi Hendrix Experience*: "Killing Floor" and "Hey Joe." The former is powerful, but "Hey Joe" sounds somewhat raggedy and features an alarmingly feminine shriek of "Hey!" from Hendrix at one point. Nonetheless, both renditions are impressive for a band that was, at the time, less than a fortnight old.

recording begins

THE EXPERIENCE RETURNED TO LONDON. On the following Sunday, October 23, they entered a studio for the first time as a group to record what would be their introduction to the world: "Hey Joe." Redding and Mitchell must have been impressed that they were already making a recording just over two weeks after their new band's formation. Also impressive to them was the fact that the three members of the band were on a wage of £15 each per week, not only a tidy sum for members of a group with no track record, but about double the wages of the average working man.

Though the story told in "Hey Joe" can be traced back several generations, the melody and lyric of this variation were recent creations. Yet for a contemporary composition, it already had a remarkably tortuous history. It was written, by a young man named Billy Roberts, on a beach—literally on a beach: he scrawled the lyric into sand—in Maine. After transferring to paper what he could remember of his take on the tale of a man who shoots his girlfriend after finding out she has been unfaithful to him, Roberts seems not to have realized the potential of the composition: he did not record it and even sold the copyright on it to one Dino Valenti, also known as Chester Powers. When both Love and the Leaves proceeded to have minor hits with "Hey Joe," and Hendrix a major one, the authorship of the song became a relevant issue. (The Byrds also released a version, on album, in 1966.) Martin Cohen, a lawyer working for publishers Third Story Music, went to visit Valenti, who was at that time serving a prison sentence in California for a drugs offense. Confronted over the issue, Valenti backed down and admitted he had no hand in the writing of "Hey Joe." It's fortunate that Roberts was able to get this issue settled and enjoy the royalties from his creation because, amazingly, he never wrote anything else of significance.

The version that Hendrix had been performing was, in fact, an arrangement devised by Tim Rose. This arrangement boasted the same intensity as the other recordings of the song, but took the tempo down to create a brooding ambience. "That was directly from me," remembers Linda Keith of Hendrix covering the song. "I played him the Tim Rose [version]. He'd never heard it. I had it as a promotional release through Keith [Richards]. Keith would get all kinds of stuff. I was playing it to everybody and they were going mad about it." Rose, who would meet Hendrix the following March at London's Speakeasy, would later say, "They did the same arrangement almost, putting Hendrixisms in it." Though Rose wasn't entitled to any remuneration for the adaptation of his arrangement—a matter of no little anguish to him—Hendrix was generous in acknowledging his debt to Rose. When promoting the record, he said to one journalist, "Lots of people have done different arrangements of it and Timmy Rose was the first to do it slowly. I like it played slowly. There are probably a thousand different versions of it fast."

For Hendrix and Chandler, there was never a question that any other song would be recorded as the Experience's debut. "They came back from America with that in mind," recalls Etchingham. Redding says, "It was him and Chas who liked the tune. I'd never heard it before. He took down the tempo compared to Tim Rose's version and he sung it differently and it was a completely different feel."

The studio chosen for the Experience's recording of "Hey Joe" was De Lane Lea Studios, in Kingsway, London. The studio (often referred to simply as Kingsway) was one with which Chandler was more than familiar: many of the Animals' recordings had been made there. De Lane Lea was one of a new breed of studios that had sprung up in the capital over the last couple of years. Successful rock musicians were becoming less prepared to put up with a studio recording scene that was characterized by conservative attitudes and a lack of a service industry outlook. Until about 1964, the only state of the art four-track studios available for those who wanted to record in London (which basically meant anyone in the United Kingdom who wanted to record) were the ones run by the major record labels: EMI (Abbey Road), Decca (Hampstead), and Pye and Phillips (both near Marble Arch). Such studios were frequently akin to aircraft hangers, designed as they were for orchestral work. De Lane Lea was deliberately designed for recording rock and roll, something that more than compensated for its relative smallness. Unlike, say, Abbey Road, it didn't consist of separate studios but of a single recording space, which was long and galley-like. "It was grand," remembers Redding of his first taste of recording with the Experience, although he points out that both he and Mitchell had recorded in studios before. "I found De Lane Lea really good, personally."

The engineer for the session was Dave Siddle, who had acted as engineer on Animals recordings. Animals drummer John Steel remembers Siddle as "middle class, unboisterous.

Could've passed as [an] industrial chemist or something. Dave Siddle was very English. He was very competent and unflappable in the studio." The role reversal with Siddle must have been somewhat strange for Chandler in his first attempt at production. Not that Chandler was the kind of man inclined to betray a lack of confidence. Yet the outspoken manager was far from dictatorial in the studio. While Redding acknowledges that Chandler's experience recording with the Animals—an archetypal one-take band—made him a firm believer in acting in a brisk and businesslike manner in the studio ("All he wanted to get down was a good backing track and then get Hendrix to sing it and put on a guitar solo and mix it") he also asserts, "Chas never really got in our way. He knew exactly what he was doing and what he wanted. He was wonderful. It was only after Chas left that the band fell apart." Chris Stamp adds, "Chas had production ideas and things but he was pretty new at producing himself. . . . The great thing about being in the studio with the producer was how well the producer created the space for you to really do your best work. So he knew that bit. In that sense, he was very right for Jimi because he wasn't saying to Jimi, 'You should play like that.' He was just creating this space and letting Jimi go wherever he liked—and then perhaps pulled him back a bit."

Chandler later claimed that at this first session, he and Hendrix had a blowup that resulted in him proffering Hendrix's passport and telling him to go back to America, to Hendrix's amusement. "That's a load of rubbish," claims Etchingham, a woman whose fondness for Chandler doesn't preclude her being well aware of the man's ability to embellish truth. "The only shouting that went on in that session was when I opened the studio door. I ruined the take and they had to do it again 'cos I opened the studio door while the red light was on. It was Chas doing the shouting. It was shouting at me, not Jimi." Redding also recalls Chandler's reaction to Etchingham's ruination of a take: "He went a bit insane."

Surviving tapes from this session reveal one accomplished (except for some overly lugubrious bass) rendition of the song. Hendrix executes a jangly guitar finale. Another take breaks down after about a minute and a half ("Try again," instructs Chandler). A further take produced the master basic track, although another basic track would be recorded at a later date before it was decided to settle for this one.

"We did quite a few takes of 'Hey Joe' and eventually we got a good backing track," says Redding. There was only one problem: "Hendrix was still trying not to sing. Chas had to turn the lights off in the studio and we got his vocal down." Hendrix's vocals on this day were also deemed unsatisfactory and were later rerecorded.

A female vocal group called the Breakaways added the dramatic background harmonies to the song. "Chas thought of that," says Redding. "They came in and did that at the end after we'd got it together." Recalls Etchingham, "Chas was holding up pieces of paper with the words on for them to sing." Redding adds, "They were professional people: they just did oohs and aahs and got it very quickly."

There may have been another song recorded at this session. Redding's diary entry for the day says: "Recording. Did two numbers." The other track may have been a version of

"Killing Floor," which Hendrix had wanted to put on the first single's B-side. "Land of 1,000 Dances," which Chandler later claimed Hendrix considered for the flip, is another contender for the mystery track. Redding's overall impression of the Experience's first recording session, as recorded in his diary, was, "Used Chas's bass. Sounded good at the session today."

The following evening, Hendrix jammed—on bass—at Knuckles Club with Deep Feeling, which included Dave Mason and Jim Capaldi, who would form one half of Traffic the following year. It was on this same day, according to Chandler, that Hendrix wrote "Stone Free," the song that would end up as the B-side to "Hey Joe." Hendrix had spoken of recording a cover as the flip side of his prospective debut, but Chandler would have none of it, telling him that there was nothing going on the B-side except one of the artist's own songs. "Chandler said to James, 'You've got to write your own stuff,'" recalls Redding. "'Cos he knew about it—publishing, that sort of crap. So he started writing." Etchingham confirms this: "Chas told him, write your own songs, 'cos that's where the money is."

It would seem that Hendrix didn't consider his meager number of pre-England compositions to be "proper" songs. The fact that Chandler was, and Etchingham and Stamp still seem to be, under the impression that Hendrix had written nothing before "Stone Free" indicates that Hendrix never told them he had and that Hendrix therefore discounted those songs. That Chandler assumed he had written nothing thus far, incidentally, raises the interesting question of what Chandler thought he had signed in the first place. Had he merely imagined selling Hendrix to the public as a virtuoso interpreter of other people's songs? From his own friends in music industry circles, Chandler would have been aware that there was no guarantee Hendrix could write just because he could make his guitar sing: there were incredibly gifted instrumentalists, such as Jeff Beck and (to a lesser extent) Eric Clapton, who were mystifyingly unable to transfer their skills on the instrument to writing original melodies. "There was no reason to know that he could," concedes Etchingham. "That's why he did 'Hey Joe': [it was a] a ready-made song which was not known in this country. Chas had only met Jimi a few weeks beforehand and then he'd gone on tour and then sort of collected him on the way back. So Chas couldn't possibly have known that he could write songs."

For Chris Stamp, though, that Hendrix would be able to compose in some way was a given: "Chas had this song which wasn't written by Jimi, and immediately Kit and I came into the picture we started to talk to Jimi—and to Chas—about songs because we related our experiences with Pete Townshend. When we signed the Who, Pete had only written one song and the Who certainly didn't perform it. I wasn't looking for a great guitar virtuoso. What touched me about rock and roll was the phenomena of it, and the idea of composing was vital to me. I wasn't trying to sign and manage or create [merely] a great guitarist. I hadn't any interest in that." The unprolific examples of Clapton and Beck didn't matter: "I personally felt someone who had such a musical gift as Jimi would certainly be able to at least transpose that into songs. What I didn't know, and became clear very quickly, was whether or not there was going to be a lyrical content there." For Stamp, lack of the latter would have posed no profound problems: "I was involved in the creative process. We could all try this. If nothing else, I could have said to Pete [Townshend], 'Hey, try to write some lyrics to Jimi's music' or something. We could have done thousands of things." Fortunately, Hendrix managed to justify—triumphantly—the faith Stamp had in him. "Even in the first couple of weeks of knowing Jimi, one saw that there was this very deeply shy, guarded man but who was a gigantic creative force—and of course he could write songs."

In fact, every single track on *Are You Experienced* (U.K. edition) would be a Hendrix original. "Once he started writing, he kept on writing," remembers Redding. "Once you get into writing, it's quite hard to get out of it. On the road, he'd be constantly scribbling lyrics, not with chords but just lyrics, which is the best way to write anyway." This method of writing may have been the source of stories, which Etchingham believes are erroneous, that Hendrix's songs were poems to which he added melodies. "Not that I know of," she says of the poems theory. "He certainly didn't have any with him when he came."

On October 25, 1966, the Jimi Hendrix Experience—as opposed to Jimi jamming with others—made its London debut. Almost inevitably, it was at the Scotch of St. James. For Redding, this was the start of the very pleasant sensation of being the center of attention. All the people who had previously been his heroes were now treating his own band reverentially. "When we got back [from France], the word was getting about about the band and that's when we started doing the clubs, and that's when we started noticing the Beatles would turn up, there'd be Bill Wyman, there'd be

Beck, whatever. Chas knew all these people himself and Chas had this flat up by Marble Arch and I always remember going up there some night after some gig and I'm sitting on the bed beside Paul McCartney, smoking a joint. And I was, like, 20 years old." For Hendrix, of course, the attention was no less pleasurable. "I think he was chuffed to have all these stars talking to him," says Redding. "And he really liked England."

For Hendrix, all this attention—adulation, even—from his peers must have been dizzying. In America, he'd been merely a sideman for established acts. In London, he was the hub of the universe, the man of whom guitarists including Eric Clapton and Jeff Beck, already well on their own way to living legend status, were in awe. The admiration wasn't restricted to his fellow guitarists. Eric Burdon idolized Hendrix from the first moment they met and referred to him in two Animals songs of the period. "You can't believe how enamored Eric was with Jimi," remembers Burdon's colleague Vic Briggs. "No words can describe how he was taken with this guy." Yet, to his credit, there was no ballooning of Hendrix's ego. Asked whether he thought he was the best guitarist around, Etchingham replies, "I think he did, definitely, although he was very humble about it." Even the accolades he was awarded by superstars such as Clapton, McCartney, and Brian Jones were worn lightly. "I think he was quite pleased, but he never talked about it," says Etchingham. "He wasn't the sort of person to brag and say, 'They all love me.' That wasn't in his repertoire. He took it all in his stride."

When it comes to the specifics of Hendrix's technique, Roger Mayer, who supplied him with his guitar gadgets, says, "One thing that's underestimated about Jimi: Jimi, if you listen, is not really a blindingly quick guitar player across the fretboard—in other words, he's not like, say, Satriani or some of these other players who play very, very quickly—but Jimi was extremely fast horizontally going up and down the guitar. In other words, changing the position on the guitar very, very quick. There's not many guitar players who are quick like that, which means that they can play chords, not in the same position on the neck, but up and down the neck, extraordinarily quickly. Jimi was probably the master of that one."

For Redding, it was Hendrix's versatility that was most extraordinary: "He was playing rhythm–lead, which is rather good. Doing intros and then going into the vocal playing rhythm and going—zip—into the solo."

Vic Briggs has profound reservations about the way Hendrix is frequently described as a genius (as does everyone else questioned for this book) and even goes so far as to say, "He was good, but he didn't have an exceptional technique. . . . Which is not to detract from his abilities, which were enormous, and the fact that he did it means that he did it and obviously I didn't, but I never looked at Jimi and said, 'I wish I could do that.'" However, he has no doubt about one undeniable musical contribution of Hendrix's: the blowing away of notions about what was possible on an electric guitar. "He may have been the first guy I ever saw who used this overdriven tone on an amplifier," he says. "In those days, guitar amplifiers were made to not distort. There wasn't any such thing as a distorted sound, except people had just started to use fuzzboxes. But if you took them way up to the top of their level then they would start to break up and the sound would be more fluid. The guitar is essentially a staccato instrument. It's a plucked instrument, and very few plucked instruments have a sustained sound, but when it's overdriven, when it starts to distort a little bit, it becomes more fluid-ey. The sound sustains longer and in actual fact it becomes more enjoyable and easier to play. But I didn't know that at the time. I was a bit of a purist."

It's possible that Hendrix was unorthodox in his approach to playing guitar not just because of a visionary's talent but because of a couple of accidents of nature: being born left-handed and possessing extraordinarily large hands that boasted thumbs as long as his fingers. Regarding those huge paws, Redding recalls, "He'd play an F sharp using his thumb, which was completely unheard of. He did have very big hands and they were all over the place. He probably used more inversions than switching chords. If you're playing an F sharp—which "Foxy Lady" was in—in the normal shape, then if you play a B shape, still using the F sharp note with your thumb, that's called an inversion. It's an F to a B, you don't have to use your hands that much. You just move your fingers a little bit."

"The acceptable or orthodox way of playing the guitar," notes Briggs, "is you keep your thumb firmly behind the neck and you don't use it at all. But he chose to do stuff: wrapping his thumb around the neck, fretting the bass strings with his thumb on occasion. Of course, when you have a new weapon in your arsenal, so to speak, your technique changes." Mayer points out: "Having a fairly large hand that goes 'round the guitar easier and a big thumb means that you can use it on the two bass strings quite easily, which Jimi did."

Hendrix's deployment of upside-down right-handed guitars seems to be due simply to technical deficiencies in left-handed instruments of the day (though Mayer says an upside-down Stratocaster has an intriguingly different tone, which Hendrix might have been aware of). However, even this happenstance resulted in ground breaking. As Redding points out: "The tremolo arm—which is now called the whammy bar—it would be by his left hand, so he could be playing away and use the tremolo bar at the same time, 'cause it was just there by the strings. On a left-handed guitar, it would have been on the other side of the strings, so he basically got used to it." The tremolo arm is used to produce vibrato by rapidly but slightly altering the pitch of any sustained note. The most famous exponent of the resulting "wavy" sound was the Shadows' Hank Marvin. "I think, before Jimi, people looked on the tremolo with disdain because Hank Marvin used it," says Briggs. "For example, the Les Pauls didn't have a tremolo arm, and that was a point of pride that the real blues players don't use tremolos, blah blah blah. The Brit players were very myopic. It was more to prove that they weren't this than they were that. Those guys who did, used it very conservatively. Well, Jimi wasn't conservative in anything, so all of a sudden he was just doing things that nobody had thought of doing before." Before long, the purists who disdained the whammy bar before Hendrix's arrival were all attempting to emulate the newcomer's tremolo tricks.

Unlike Linda Keith, Etchingham doesn't remember Hendrix incessantly playing his instrument. When Chandler's claim that Hendrix would even fry eggs with a Strat round his neck is put to her, she scoffs: "Not *that* much. Sometimes he would tring away for some time, then other times he never picked the guitar up at all." Hendrix had no specific schedule for practice, either. "Definitely not," she recalls. "When the mood took him. Then he'd sit there for quite some time." Nor was Hendrix precious about his practice: "He could do it in front of the TV. He didn't have to sit that quietly." Any practice in the early days in Britain was electric practice. "In the summer of '67, he got an acoustic guitar, an Epiphone," says Etchingham, "which he bought in New York. [He] brought that back and he used that continuously."

Hendrix, of course, had partly acquired his huge talent by sitting at the metaphorical feet of his own axe heroes. "When it came to guitar," Etchingham reveals, "his old favorites were Elmore James, B. B. King, Howlin' Wolf, Robert Johnson, John Lee Hooker." Hendrix would combine those fairly predictable blues influences with ones whom it was very unusual for a black artist—and almost unthinkable for a black consumer—to admire. Linda Keith has already noted the influence of Bob Dylan. "Bob Dylan was his all-time favorite, as far as lyrics were concerned," confirms Etchingham. "He loved Bob Dylan." Redding also points out, "He liked the English music scene at that point—like the Move, the Small Faces, et cetera, et cetera. Pop/rock, as they called it."

Then there were the Beatles. Hendrix would list the Fab Four as one of his favorite groups in teen magazine features (as did everyone else). He was also impressed enough by *Sgt. Pepper's Lonely Hearts Club Band* the following year to open the Experience's set with its title track three days after the album's release. Their biggest effect on Hendrix, however, was probably via osmosis, and it was revolutionary. The lead guitar/rhythm guitar/bass/drums group format that the Liverpudlians had made almost a compulsory template for a rock group was actually quite unusual for the black tradition from which Hendrix came. Instead of a second guitar, saxophones or pianos were more likely instruments to be found on the chitlin circuit. When Hendrix chose to use that format with the Experience (handling both rhythm and lead guitarist roles himself), Jimi Hendrix became the first black *rock* star, as opposed to R & B star (like Bo Diddley), soul star (like Otis Redding), or rock 'n' roll star (like Little Richard and Chuck Berry). In other words, he was the first black frontman of a Beatles-format group that played rock and pop. Musically, this distinction may be irrelevant. Culturally, it was of vast significance. So was the mixed-race makeup of the Experience, which was unique in Britain, although there were similar configurations in the States (such as the band Love).

Some have contended that the Jimi Hendrix Experience was purely Hendrix, and that his backing musicians were unimportant. Nik Cohn—usually an intelligent commentator on rock—has even gone so far as to state that Mitchell and Redding have no real right to complain about the paucity of royalties they received as a consequence of the bad management of the band's finances, and that they were lucky to get what they did. This is so wrongheaded as to defy belief. The Jimi Hendrix Experience was always more than Hendrix. This was a great *band*, one that simply would not have made music as fine as it did had it consisted of Hendrix backed by two pedestrian hacks, or even two other virtuosos. Proof of this is provided by the several bands Hendrix played with outside the Experience—the Band of Gypsys, the Gypsys, Sons & Rainbows Band, and the Cry of Love Band—all, though possibly technically superior to the Experience, sound unimaginative, even drab, in comparison to the performances and recordings of the original Experience trio.

Auger applauds not just the technical proficiency of the Experience, but its unusualness: "I think that early trio was just a very different approach. It was only in England that something like that could happen. When Jimi came to the States, the choice of Billy Cox and Buddy Miles—tremendous players as they are—that was much more of an orthodox rhythm section for music like that." However, his admiration for the Experience is not unequivocal: "I think the bass player was a strange choice. There were plenty of people who were much stronger than he was at the time. What can I say? The band works." It should be pointed out that Auger's comments about Redding's abilities are somewhat undermined when he states how much he enjoyed the basslines on *Are You Experienced* and then reveals that he is under the (erroneous) impression that Hendrix was responsible for playing many of them.

Charles Shaar Murray, author of a book-length critique of Hendrix's music, makes an interesting observation about Redding's role: "Somebody had to hold things down. He was very solid. He didn't have the fluency or the imagination of either Bruce or [John] Entwistle, but Hendrix probably needed somebody in the band who wasn't an off-the-wall virtuoso. Somebody who would stay on the one. 'Cos if the drums are going out there and the guitar's going out there, you can't have the bass player going out there as well. That's actually why a lot of Cream's long improvisations I don't think have stood the test of time—because *everybody* was out there. Nobody was actually playing the beat anymore."

Vic Briggs has no reservations about Redding: "He was a lead guitar player. He did things on the bass that people wouldn't normally do. It wasn't like he was playing lead bass, but he was ready to expand out and open up in a technical way that most bass players wouldn't. When you come to an instrument without the preconceived notions that you get from being trained in that instrument, sometimes you can do surprising things. More from the records than the live work was where I noticed that."

Though very cohesive onstage, the individual members of the Experience were able to survive without each other. "I don't think they socialized an awful lot outside the band, in fact, I know they didn't," says Etchingham. "They used to run their own lives. They weren't always together." Not that this implies any particular tensions: "They did get on tremendously well," says Chris Welch. "I used to see them backstage at gigs and stuff and they were always laughing and joking and fooling around. So it was a good vibe within the band."

From Redding's point of view, the vital fourth member of the Experience was Chandler. "I just think we were all in the right place at the right time," he says. "It was a black American guitar player with two white guys and Chas, who'd been about, knew what he was doing when he produced us, and he was a wonderful manager. You'd never see Jeffries [sic] at any gig, but Chandler would come to the gigs and hang out. We'd have a pint. He was one of the lads. After any gig, Jimi, Chas and I would actually go through it. An after-gig chat. We just progressed very, very quickly."

On October 29, 1966, the Experience notched up an important milestone by receiving its first mention in the U.K. music press, albeit a slightly farcical one. *Record Mirror* reported, "Chas Chandler has signed and brought to this country a 20 [sic]-year-old Negro called Jim [sic] Henrix [sic] who, among other things, plays the guitar with his teeth and is being hailed in some quarters as main contender for the title of 'the next big thing.'"

Though Etchingham and Redding insist that the Experience's attitude regarding rehearsals was perfunctory, to say the least, in the early days there does seem to have been some attempt made to do the conventional thing and work through numbers. The late Vivian Price, sometime member of the Pretty Things, has recalled Chandler asking in October 1966 if the band could rehearse in his Knuckles club when it was closed in the afternoons. Price obliged and later reported that Hendrix used a small cassette recorder to capture every number and play it back to see how it sounded.

Sometime before the end of October, Chandler, Hendrix, and an unknown female backing vocal trio visited Pye Studios in London for more work on "Hey Joe." Redding's and Mitchell's presence was not required for what was a lead and backing vocal overdub session on the October 23 basic track. Pye was a prestigious studio which, as well as playing host to pop stars such as the Kinks, was also a venue for much orchestral work. Like De Lane Lea, the recording space consisted of a single large room, although this one was square shaped. A surviving outtake from this session reveals Hendrix fluffing his lines immediately after the first "Hey Joe." He then explodes, "Oh God . . . damn!," laughing. He continues attempting to sing until the end of the track, presumably either to familiarize himself with it or so that bits of his vocal can be plucked for use on the master. This version, inevitably scrapped, can be heard on the 2000 CD box set *The Jimi Hendrix Experience* (though its annotation is inadvertently misleading, omitting any reference to De Lane Lea and thus giving the impression that a new basic track was recorded at Pye). The female vocals are more prominent and ethereal than on the familiar version of the song, and the track ends with a clatter of drums, not the fade out ultimately chosen.

At some point in the first couple of months of the band's existence, Hendrix tinkered with the setup of the Experience by rehearsing another bass player. Most reference books cite this happening in mid-November 1966, though Redding thinks it was in October, and after the "Hey Joe" recording session on the 23rd. "The idea was," Redding explains, "he'd [Jimi] play lead guitar, I'd play rhythm guitar—or we'd swap." The man they rehearsed was David Knights, later of Procol Harum. The audition didn't work out, although the fact that Hendrix didn't audition anyone else would indicate that it wasn't due to dissatisfaction with Knights. "Hendrix, after, [said,] 'No, we should stick to three-piece,'" recalls Redding. "I said, 'Yeah.'"

toward a record deal

ON NOVEMBER 1, THE EXPERIENCE rehearsed at Aberbach. The following day saw the Experience returning to De Lane Lea Studios from 6:00 P.M. to 12:00 P.M. to record the B-side to "Hey Joe," "Stone Free," as well as a rough demo of "Can You See Me" (which has remained unreleased). There may have been another track attempted: Redding's diary entry reads: "Did three numbers." Chandler would later say of "Stone Free," "I couldn't afford to have the band learn the song in the studio, so I booked a rehearsal at the Aberbach House beforehand." Chandler would soon realize that the extraordinary abilities of the Experience made this kind of preparation unnecessary.

Hendrix's first proper song turned out to have a vehement message in favor of personal freedom, one that seemed to preclude long-term relationships with female partners. Etchingham might have been expected to be alarmed by the lyric to "Stone Free"—even though she has admitted that her relationship with Hendrix was never monogamous on either side—but she says that she thought nothing of it: "There's so many songs like that. People sing all kinds of things. Look at all his other songs, how they change from one thing to another. Just a turn of the songwriter's pen, really. I don't think you can read too much into them." She also adds, "When people asked him what his words meant in the songs, he used to get quite flustered, 'cos he didn't really know himself."

In the second week of November, the Experience played on several consecutive days at the Big Apple in Munich, performing two shows each night. Redding cites the events that occurred at one of these gigs as the start of Hendrix's musical love affair with feedback: "Hendrix got pulled off the stage by the crowd. So what he did, he threw his guitar back on the stage because he didn't want to harm it. They let him back on stage, by which time the guitar was feeding back. I think that's probably the first time he sort of realized what could happen. Mitch and I were still playing, just ad-libbing. So then Hendrix, he just let it feed back."

On November 18, yet more work was done on "Hey Joe," this time at Regent Sound Studio on Tottenham Court Road, London. This session seems to have been a rerecording of the basic track rather than overdub work. A version of "Hey Joe" that continues to float around the bootleg circuit is thought to be from this session. It features some perfunctory singing from Hendrix and a rather limp guitar solo. Understandably, it was never used.

Also not used—at least during Hendrix's lifetime—was "Here He Comes," one of two songs the Experience record-ed on November 24, from 2:00 P.M. to 5:00 P.M., this time at De Lane Lea. The other track recorded that day was "Love or Confusion." It seems reasonable to assume that by now the Experience was aware that they were making an album, but it's difficult to cite which recording date constituted the first *Are You Experienced* session. The November 1 session was the first one at which tracks that would end up on the album were recorded—but it could be that these tracks were all originally intended for release on either the A- or B-sides of singles, just as it could that these tracks recorded on the 24th was. It's only by looking at the number of songs the band was stockpiling that one can gauge that their intentions were by this point LP-oriented.

"Here He Comes" seems to have been a real creative monkey on Hendrix's back. A Hendrix original that was inspired by B. B. King's "Rock Me Baby," it was played on stage by Hendrix in every band he performed with. Hendrix repeatedly attempted to produce a satisfactory recorded version, yet it was never released in any form until after Hendrix's death, when a live version appeared on the *Isle of Wight* album, by which time it had been rechristened "Lover Man." Though Redding can't remember the specifics of recording this track, he states that Chandler was always able to prevent the Experience from getting hung up on a track that wasn't working: "He wouldn't tell us what to do, but he would advise: 'Well, that needs a little bit more work on it and we've got a demo of it now, so we can try it again next time.' That sort of stuff. That's where Chandler was so good."

Chandler's precaution of having the Experience rehearse "Stone Free" before recording it proved to be unnecessary. Much of *Are You Experienced* was taught to Redding and Mitchell in the studio, but the amount this added to the recording costs was negligible due to the group's extraordinary capacity to learn a song inside out by the time they'd gone through a couple of run-throughs. In this they were assisted by Hendrix, who would have already done considerable work on arrangements with Chandler at their shared domicile. (Chandler has recalled being part of the process, watching the guitarist at work and guiding him by commenting when he felt Hendrix had hit on something good.) Hendrix invited his new colleagues to fly by the seat of their pants when adding their contributions. Redding: "Mitch would be setting up. Hendrix and I would sit in the corner with two guitars and I'd just get him to teach me the chords, then we'd take it. I used to learn the chords off him on a guitar because it was quicker and I'd just play it on the bass."

Etchingham, who attended many of the album's sessions, recalls Hendrix's masterful control of this organized mayhem: "Jimi behaved like a conductor. He used to turn 'round and tap Mitch's cymbal . . . with the butt of his guitar . . . to indicate, 'This is it. Finished.' Or nod to him or make gestures." As a graduate of the slap-it-down-and-whack-it-out-into-the-marketplace school of recording, Chandler was, of course, all in favor of this labor-light method. "We'd just go through it a couple of times to get the chords and the feel and Chandler, without telling us, would put the tape on," recalls Redding.

The following day, an Experience press reception and concert took place at the Bag O' Nails. This lavish event was the latest step in Chandler's strategy to display Hendrix to the pop cognoscenti. Though this strategy had potentially high rewards, it also had high risks: Chandler, who had already spent much of his not very considerable resources on recording, had to sell some of his possessions to pay for the event. "Money was always a problem," says Etchingham. "November of 1966 we were completely broke." Chandler would later claim that he sold five of his own guitars to pay for the Bag O' Nails event. "I think it was one of Chas's exaggerations there," says Etchingham. "He probably sold one or two, but I don't think he sold five. I don't think he *had* five!"

In Etchingham's opinion, the Bag O' Nails performance

confirmed once and for all Hendrix's arrival in the musical firmament to his peers—of whom one of the most celebrated—Paul McCartney—was sitting at Etchingham's table. Other celebrities present included John Lennon, Eric Clapton, Pete Townshend, Donovan, Mick Jagger, Brian Jones, Jeff Beck, and Jimmy Page. "It was packed with them," she says. "And that was it. That was when they all thought, 'Ooh, shit! What's this?' And the acoustics in there weren't that good, either." Hendrix, resplendent in the pirate-looking Veterinary Corps jacket he'd lately taken to wearing, lived up to the occasion with a mixture of musical brilliance and showmanship. "I was sitting just at the left of the stage," says Etchingham, who found herself the target of one of Hendrix's lascivious stage gestures. "I was terribly embarrassed because Jimi did that tongue thing right at me. 'Oh *God!*'"

On the 26th, the Experience warmed up the crowd in support of the feature act, the new Animals, at the Ricky Tick Club in Hounslow, just outside London. The Animals' Vic Briggs recalls the delighted shock at Hendrix's onstage lasciviousness by one of the audience that evening: "I was there with this lady that night and after the gig, she says to me, 'Boy. That guy was so sexy.' I said, 'What guy?' She said, 'That guy who was on before you.' I says, 'You mean Jimi?' She goes, 'Yeah. God, I've never seen anybody being so sexual on stage.' I had to think about it. I was surprised, 'cos people, in those days, didn't usually say that kind of stuff in England." Of course, England would get used to Hendrix's overt stage sexuality, which included him employing his guitar as a phallic symbol—something which, back then, was enough to cause a heart attack in the non-rock strata of society. "There wasn't anybody doing stuff like that," says Briggs. "Even the crazies, guys like Screaming Lord Sutch, they never did stuff like that. You couldn't get away with it. It just wasn't done." Briggs feels that, because Hendrix was both black and American, he was allowed a certain license and that his antics were excused as exotica.

All of the excitement that Hendrix was generating among both fellow musicians and audiences must have made it mystifying to both Chandler and Hendrix that record companies didn't automatically succumb to the man's charms. Chandler took an acetate of the finished "Hey Joe" to Decca Records and was taken aback to be told they didn't think he had any potential. "It was a bit of a shocker, that was, that he was turned down by Decca," recalls Etchingham. "But they just plodded on."

Bewildering though that rejection may have been, it was perhaps the best thing that could have happened to Hendrix, for it meant the way was open for the Experience to sign with Kit Lambert and Chris Stamp as Track Records artists. It's highly possible that *Are You Experienced* would not have been the revolutionary record it was had the band signed with a conventional label such as Decca. With Track, Hendrix was guaranteed complete artistic freedom by people who believed without equivocation in the viability of his vision.

"At that time, independent record labels were really needed," says Stamp. The new label might have remained a mere aspiration of his and Lambert's without Hendrix entering their lives. "We *had* been thinking of starting a record label, but this suddenly spurred us to begin immediately. Island was starting up, Andrew Oldham's Immediate was starting up but the record business was totally dominated by Decca and EMI and Pye and there was Phillips. It was just very formula and they was no real sense of recognizing what was happening in that era. There was no outside consciousness in these record companies." Conventional record companies, from Stamp's and Lambert's point of view, were interested in commerce first, art last. Track would reverse those priorities. Stamp: "Of course we wanted to make a lot of money, but it wasn't the be-all and end-all. Track wasn't conceived as a company that was gonna put out a gimmick record because it was gonna be a hit. It speaks for itself: we released 'Two Virgins' [under the Apple Records label] by John Lennon because no one else would. Not saying that we particularly liked the music. We did that because that's how we felt: it was a stance." The ideals behind Track were grand indeed. Stamp recites the studio's philosophy: "Rock and roll is gonna change society. We're gonna do something really serious here. We considered ourselves as valid—as filmmakers and as managers and as producers—as the artists. We were interested integrally in what he [Hendrix] had to commit to the world of music, and the world of music at the time was a sort of symbol of a much bigger change that the people of our era were struggling with. We started a record company because the record companies were, like, shit. By being an independent record company you could really follow through your ideas."

The fact that Track would be relying on a big company—Polydor—to distribute their wares was, according to Stamp, irrelevant: "We could totally control our destinies. We determined how many were pressed. Our deal with Polydor was that all of that was ours. They just had to release our product. Their side of it was the pressing, the distribution, and the accounting." Polydor was at least the best of a bad bunch: "We weren't too enamored of them, but at that time it was being run by a guy called Roland Rennie, and he had carte blanche to make deals and do things that were creative, and he was allowing us to go much further with all our ideas than any of the other companies had ever dreamed about."

It's reasonable to assume, however, that Stamp's and Lambert's grand ideals were of little consequence to Chandler and Hendrix. Their objective was to sell records, and Hendrix becoming a rich and famous star was wrapped up in that objective. Stamp had to offer the Hendrix camp something more than statements such as "Rock and roll is gonna change society." Luckily, what he and Lambert did have to offer was considerable, even though it didn't involve a large cash advance against royalties. Instead, they were able to offer Hendrix contacts, knowledge, and experience. Having their fingers in so many pop media pies and being acquainted with so many individuals who could boost Hendrix's career was arguably even more important than an injection of capital. "When we eventually got to talk to Mike and Chas about that sort of thing, we said, 'Look, we can't really come up with advances, that's not what we're doing,'" recalls Stamp. "We put our package together as a conceptual idea of what we would be able to do. What Kit and I were great at was creative thinking around the whole concept of how to launch an artist: the promotion and the way that it was looked at. So we were trying to enamor them of this idea. We said, 'We will be the record label for the world outside of the United States. We will make Jimi a star here, and then you can go to America and get this big advance that you want.' That was how we sold it to Chas and Mike. And we came up with a thousand pounds' advance as a sort of gesture of our good intention. It was *quite* a lot of money, but if you had what you thought was a hit act you could have still gone into Decca and EMI and got a lot more than that. You could certainly have got a lot more than that if you signed a world-wide deal, including America, if you had evidence that this thing looked like it was going to be a success."

On top of that was a promise that the pair would pull off the coup of getting Hendrix—who, despite being the talk of the town, was in general terms an unknown—an appearance on *Ready, Steady, Go!* This Friday night TV program was one of only a handful of shows dedicated to popular music on Britain's TV airwaves (which at that time featured only three channels, of which one—BBC2—was very highbrow). *Ready, Steady, Go!* was the most highly regarded of these shows. It had started as a lip-synched show with occasional live performances. In the early part of 1965, it became a totally live show (and even provided a studio orchestra for solo artists). This air of authenticity, its artist-friendly ambience, and its knowledgeable production team made it the favorite of the pop stars of the day. A performance on *RSG*, as the program was commonly known, of Hendrix's debut single would amount to thousands of pounds of free advertising. Stamp says that, although he didn't really have any authority to book artists for the show, he had no doubt that he could get Hendrix the gig. "We were creatively involved with every-body who ran *Ready, Steady, Go!*," he recalls. "They liked our ideas for the show. It's a creative angle. We'd given 'em a few ideas, so we knew that they would take another one of our ideas. We weren't trying to stiff them. This is all about a creative type of community. It wasn't about payola. We were filmmakers. They said, 'Of course.' Because they figured we would come up with something pretty amazing."

Stamp is insistent that it wasn't the promised appearance on *RSG* that swung it for Chandler and Jeffery, however. "It's not that simplistic," he says. "Chas and Mike really liked our managerial input around Jimi. They were getting good feedback from us. They were getting a lot of management, a lot of producing ideas, they were getting a lot of concepts—all thrown into the deal. So they realized that it wasn't necessarily gonna make a lot of money for them, but they were gonna have an incredible shot for their artist to work."

In the first week of December 1966, Hendrix, Etchingham, Chandler, and Lotta moved into Ringo Starr's vacant flat in Montagu Square, London. That Hendrix and Chandler were now not just friends and colleagues but also flatmates was not as claustrophobic a state of affairs as might be imagined. "Montagu Square was on two floors, and Chas was on one and we were on the other, so it wasn't difficult," says Etchingham. "We weren't thrown together in a small apartment. As you can imagine, Ringo Starr's flat would be [a big place]."

December 10 saw the Experience supporting John Mayall's Bluesbreakers at the Ram Jam Club in Brixton. The following day, Hendrix hooked up with his old colleague Little Richard, who was touring Britain. On their way back from Richard's hotel, Hendrix and Etchingham were subjected to some harassment from police officers who took exception to his military jacket. Hendrix's perennial politeness ensured that the incident fizzled out, but it was clear that both he and his colleagues in the Experience were developing a fashion sense that was beginning to make them stand out. "Chas wanted us to get suits," recalls Redding, "and I think Hendrix refused, and that's when he got one of those military jackets from somewhere down on the King's Road and suddenly this image of the band started appearing: I had long hair, I used to have a pair of pink jeans—which you couldn't get in those days. We just started being outrageous in our dress."

On December 13, 1966, the Experience recorded its first TV appearance—the prestigious *Ready Steady Go!* slot Stamp had thrown in as an inducement to sign with Track. Although Hendrix had appeared once on television in the States in the Little Richard days, it was his first TV appearance as a front man. One might assume it was an occasion for some nervousness on the part of the guitarist, but Etchingham claims he took it in his stride: "He was confident. He was always quite confident." Mitchell had appeared on television many times as a child actor, so was also laid back about it. This was in contrast to Redding. "I'd never done television before," Redding says. "I was terrified. We did it with the Merseys— who used to be the Merseybeats—and Keith Relf and the Yardbirds. I was just so chuffed to be on the television." The Experience played, of course, "Hey Joe," which would be released three days later. "That created the initial base, which is all we were aiming for," says Stamp. "We knew that the audience of *Ready, Steady, Go!* were musically a little bit hip. They weren't as broad as the *Top of the Pops* audience, but we knew that they would get off on Jimi."

Stamp and Lambert were also helping to arrange press

coverage. Much of this coverage portrayed Hendrix (in a perfectly nonmalicious way) as wild, primeval, and savage. At least one reporter actually referred to the guitarist as a Wild Man of Borneo. Hendrix certainly had the appearance: it's perhaps forgotten how unheard of it was for a black man to have bushy hair in the mid-1960s. With the exception of a couple of pompadours (Little Richard's being the most extravagant), black men's hairstyles were usually closely cropped at the time—a look that was invariably found on the members of soul vocal groups.

Not that Stamp and Lambert were going to complain about the way the papers chose to portray their client. "We also believed very much that any press was good press as long as you had a photograph. We didn't really care what they said." Most of the press coverage focused on Hendrix rather than the band as a whole. Stamp reasons, "We considered them a group, but we didn't consider them a group in that sense the Who were a group—*they* were very much a group. But the Jimi Hendrix Experience is what it is. It says it: Jimi Hendrix Experience."

The Experience had no time to sit back and reflect on the occasion of the recording of their inaugural TV performance. After the program, it was straight into more recording, this time at CBS Studios in London. Perhaps due to the elation of having just made their first TV appearance, they had a remarkably productive session: it's possible that "3rd Stone from the Sun," "Foxy Lady," "Can You See Me," and "Red House" were all laid down on that same day.

The CBS studio, located right in the heart of London's West End, had at one time been called Levy's Sound Studios.

Its renaming came about when the record company CBS (known as Columbia in the States) bought Oriole Records, of which the studio was a subsidiary. Like De Lane Lea and Pye, it was just one room, albeit one big enough to accommodate a 40-piece orchestra. The building had been a ballroom back in the 1920s and consequently had a very high domed ceiling. Levy's Sound Studios had installed a false ceiling made of canvas to stop splashback from the top of the dome.

The engineer assisting Chandler and the Experience during what turned out to be a short tenure at CBS was Mike Ross (now better known as Mike Ross-Trevor), a 21-year-old who had previously worked with Donovan and the Who. Ross-Trevor says that, though the studio was by now owned by a record company, it was still considered by recording artists to be an independent studio. "It was run completely separately from the main record company and we were still doing third party work, which is why we had Hendrix there," he explains. Of its facilities, he says, "It was typical of the studios of the day. The multi-track was only a four-track. Very small console. We had an EMI console, 14-channel input and four tracks out. Very basic. EQ facilities were just top and bottom, cut and boost. We had one echo plate and a natural echo room in the roof and one Fairchild compressor."

Ross-Trevor knew of Hendrix's producer: "He was in a famous band. So when the sessions came in, I recognized the name straight away. I heard he was paying for the sessions and he was coming in to record a guitarist he'd discovered in America. Nothing was out. He was a total unknown." Ross-Trevor recalls the session as being an afternoon one: "They came in about four o'clock." He remembers the Experience being very businesslike during their time at CBS, which probably explains why they made no mention to him that they had just recorded their inaugural television appearance. The businesslike manner seems to be reflected in the fact that this time there were no extraneous people such as girlfriends in the entourage, although Ross-Trevor says, "Mike Jeffries [sic] turned up at one point during the sessions." Jeffery's presence didn't seem to be to a particular purpose: "He actually didn't take much interest in the session at all. Turned up in a suit and sat there and talked like a manager. He could have been selling eggs. I think he felt as though he should just come and show his face and go."

Ross-Trevor's first impressions of Hendrix—who had arrived wearing his military jacket, looking larger than life— were much more positive. "I found him quite a shy guy," he recalls. "He was very quiet, didn't say much to anybody. But he was extremely, polite, very nice, very appreciative— always thanked you when he left, always made a point of coming in and saying hello to you." Ross-Trevor did not find anything disagreeable about Hendrix's colleagues, either: "They were fine. Mitch particularly was very nice."

Ross-Trevor was impressed by the care Mitchell took over his instrument's sound. "We had a great discussion about how to mike up drum kits on the first day. At that time, we didn't use to put a lot of mikes on the drums. There was usually one on the kick drum and one mike over the top. I remember him coming in and saying he did some sessions at Lansdowne Studios—I guess he was playing for somebody else as a session guy—and he was saying that they miked all the tom-toms up separately and put a mike on the snare and put a couple of mikes on the cymbals and he said, 'Do you fancy trying it?' I said, 'Yeah OK, I'll go along with it.' That was the first time I'd actually put more than two microphones on a drum kit. Mitch was very, very particular about his drum sound and obviously made comments and then we changed a few things, moved mikes around. Of the three of them, Mitch was probably the most particular."

As for Redding, Ross-Trevor recalls, "Noel didn't say very much at all. I don't think we had any problems with his bass sound at all. It was good, came up fine." He did notice how unusual Redding's style was: "It's a very pointed bass, very sharp. You can actually hear the notes. There's not much overtone between the strings. Which is probably why they say he plays it like a guitar. It gets a very good sound."

Hendrix, meanwhile, amazed Ross-Trevor with his equipment. "He came in with four Marshall stacks and a huge, huge amp," he says. "It was so loud you couldn't stand in the studio. It was just unbelievably loud. I'm saying, 'Where the hell am I gonna put the mike?' and he says, 'Oh, man, just put a microphone about twelve feet away on the other side of the studio. It'll sound great.' Which is what I did, using a Neumann U67 tube mike." Hendrix's prediction about what would result sonically turned out to be accurate. Ross-Trevor: "My total memory of all those sessions is just the sheer power of everything. Just how loud everything was. I'd never heard anything like it in my life."

Whether Chandler's booking studios of generous proportions for the Experience was a matter of design or chance is something that will probably never be known, but Ross-

Trevor is convinced that recording in big rooms was absolutely vital to the uniquely powerful Experience sound. "He couldn't have used a small room, because the sound wouldn't have had a chance to breathe," he points out. "They would have had to have the mike closer, which would have meant padding the microphone down, and then you would have got a smaller sound."

Ross-Trevor set up the Experience in an area where a good rhythm sound was known to result. Mitchell was located in a drum booth in the corner, with Hendrix to the left of the booth and Redding to the right. Acoustic screens were placed around the drum kit to stop the rattling noise caused by Jimi's amp setting up a vibration in the drum skins. "It was the corner that was carpeted as well," says Ross-Trevor. "'Cos the other side of the studio wasn't carpeted—it was just polished floor: we usually used that for brass and strings and stuff."

Though Hendrix would frequently issue instructions to and discuss things with Redding and Mitchell, Ross-Trevor remembers Chandler as being the one in charge, frequently leaving the control booth to go out and speak to the musicians: "There was no question about that. The other three guys didn't really have much to say and didn't really have much input. They just got on with playing." Though Ross-Trevor includes Hendrix in this description of fairly subservient behavior, he got the impression of particular subservience on the part of the rhythm section: "It was almost as though Hendrix was the star and Noel and Mitch were like the session guys hired for the gig. That's the impression I got, even back then. I never once felt this was a band. It was Hendrix and two session guys."

The Experience members played as if they were on stage. Ross-Trevor: "The track was done live, everybody playing together." He adds, however, "There was no live vocals at all." Accustomed to helping arrange multiple guitar overdubs for the Who, Ross-Trevor was surprised to find that the Experience preferred to iron out problems organically. "We burnt a lot of tape and we were doing take after take after take before we got the definitive version," he recalls. "And there didn't seem to be any talk about doing edits. They kept going until they got a great performance. There was never any talk about, 'Let's take a piece from take two and another piece from take five.' I think Chas Chandler was after the feel. I don't think he was after anything technically perfect." Though the Experience was doing more than the two or three takes of a song Ross was used to, he also recalls that they didn't need to do more than six or seven. Not that this was due to any limit being put on take numbers. To his credit, Chandler—skirting virtual bankruptcy at this stage—was happy to have the band spend as long as they needed on a song, something that would be a contrast to other sessions for the album. "He certainly wasn't clock watching," says Ross-Trevor.

Overdubs were not much of an issue with a guitarist like Hendrix, who could switch from rhythm playing (playing multiple strings at the same time, usually in a stabbed style, to help maintain the beat) to lead work (which is usually more sinuous than rhythm work and employs one string at a time—with which a musician decorates a track) so effortlessly. "And he could switch from sound to sound as well," says Ross-Trevor. "You could be playing and suddenly you get a completely different sound. You didn't have to overdub it. It wasn't, 'Oh, I have to overdub this part 'cos I can't switch it quick enough,' which is what you get with most people." The impression of a concert performance transplanted to a recording studio was completed by Hendrix making journeys to his amplifiers: "He fiddled with the control a lot, which is something you don't normally see. There'd be a break in the guitar and Mitch would be doing a fill or something and he would dash over to the amp and turn knobs and things."

Ross-Trevor's recollection is that two rhythm tracks were laid down at this first session and two more at the next, which was on the 15th. Some books have claimed that Mitchell didn't show up for the session on the 15th, but Ross-Trevor has no recollection of this, and Redding's diary entry for that date is ambiguous about whether it was a rehearsal or a recording session that Mitchell absented himself from. Such was the briefness of the band's stay at the studio, however, that it can be said with certainty that all four of the tracks recorded at CBS were laid down by the 15th.

"3rd Stone from the Sun" resulted from one of the few passions in Hendrix's life other than his music. "He used to read science fiction all the time," explains Redding. "So did Chandler." Etchingham, however, adds, "I don't remember him sitting reading for great long periods of time, so I don't know where he read these books. He must have read a few, but he wasn't an avid reader by any stretch of the imagination." According to Chandler, Hendrix based the lyric of this track on the science fiction novel *Earth Abides* by George R. Stewart, which Chandler had lent him. The book, which follows the adventures of a man who finds himself immune to a plague that has wiped out almost all of the rest of the human race, is considered a classic of the genre. As the lyric of "3rd Stone. . ." actually concerns a spaceship that comes to Earth and finds it so lacking in discernible value—apart from its superior cackling hen—that it decides to destroy it, it's difficult to see the connection with Stewart's work. In any case, as Redding points out, the lyric is not the fulcrum of the composition: "We just put down the track and he put down those funny vocals in the background. It's basically an instrumental with a verbal on top of it."

Ross-Trevor actually believes that the composition (which was ultimately rerecorded; this version was not used) would have been better without the multitudinous effects added to the mix at Olympic on a later date: "I thought it was better in its raw state. I actually quite like that raw sound—just the three of them, and maybe a vocal stuck on top. I think it has far more impact. The more things you stick on, I think it takes away the power of the three of them playing together, 'cos it reduces in volume 'cos you gotta get all the other stuff in there. That's why some of the outtakes you hear of Hendrix are very good." One thing about "3rd Stone. . ." that was retained from this first stab, however, is its unusual playing time: "Very long," recalls Ross-Trevor. "May even have been longer. I remember it went on forever."

Something indistinguishably similar to the hypnotic, exotic refrain of this song appeared on Cozy Powell's 1974 U.K. Top Five hit "Dance with the Devil." The lyric is also said to have been a source of inspiration to a different type of artist, although this is highly debatable. A July 1969 edition of the comic book *Donald Duck*, scripted and drawn by Carl

Barks, featured a story called "Officer for a Day," in which the speech-impaired Disney character gets to be a cop for one shift. One of the problems he has to deal with is a flying saucer manned by beings who assume that chickens are the Earth's dominant life form. Despite the similarity of plot, Barks expert Gerd Syllwasschy has his doubts about a Hendrix connection, pointing out that Barks was then 67 years old and an arch conservative.

Although the take of "3rd Stone. . ." laid down at CBS was ultimately scrapped, the Experience got "Foxy Lady" right then and there. The track would subsequently have overdubs added to it, but the basic track of the opening cut of (the U.K.) *Are You Experienced* was perfected in one CBS session. It has been suggested that Hendrix wrote "Foxy Lady" as a lecherous tribute to Heather Taylor, who would later marry the Who's Roger Daltrey. Daltrey confirms the story. "We was all hanging out together—and she was the unattainable one," he laughs. "She went out with me instead." In addition to his bass playing, Redding made another musical contribution to the track: "They couldn't think of an ending. It was in F sharp. I said, 'Play a B,' and we ran through the ending and they kept the B in."

Following the rough demo they had made of the track on November 2, the Experience pursued "Can You See Me" at CBS until they nailed it, producing the track that would be used—with some later overdubs—as the master. The outtakes impressively display how quickly this very young band could now iron out the creases in a track. Early versions are stiff, and the now famous flamenco riffs of Hendrix's are nothing like the fluid sounds found on the master. Yet by the end of the session, the band had produced the basic track of the rendition we know and love. Though he recalls that the basic track was completed, Ross-Trevor says, "That was the one that they didn't actually do anything to. They just did the basic track and they wanted to come back and finish it. [Hendrix] did the vocals on the other three, but not that one." He adds, "It's possible he could have put a rough down, but I don't think I did the final vocal unless they used the rough vocal."

As if all that wasn't enough, the CBS tenure also saw the recording—from beginning to end—of the magnificent "Red House"—that is, the U.K. version of "Red House," so called because it appeared on the British version of *Are You Experienced*, but not the American. The first American taste of this song was via a different version, recorded later in the sessions, that was released on the American edition of the Hendrix compilation *Smash Hits* in 1969.

An alternate mix of this U.K. version reveals some comments from Chandler that illustrate the advantages of living in the same flat as your producer. He can be heard saying, "Jimi, do you wanna thrash around with that 'Red House' thing you were messing around with this afternoon at the flat and we'll put it down for a laugh, see what it sounds like, eh?" The fact that it was Chandler making the suggestion suggests that, just possibly, it might not have occurred to Hendrix to record a song that was very conventional compared to the other material he was now writing. For this rendition, which would display arguably the most stunning, supple-wristed virtuosity of Hendrix's career, Noel Redding—who had learned about the blues from the Burnettes, who played it in

Germany to please American GIs—had a suggestion that resulted in the track featuring no bass whatsoever: "I thought a guitar would be better on it and I borrowed this guitar somewhere—I think it was Bill Wyman's or someone's—and I put it right onto a bassy sound through the amp. And it worked. Having a rhythm guitar with the lead guitar was much more subtle than putting a bass on it." Redding feels that even without Hendrix's lightning-flash runs, "Red House" would still be something more than a generic exercise: "I just thought the vibe was good on the tune and also it was in B, which not many people can play in."

Interestingly, though outtakes reveal the American version of "Red House" to have a live vocal, Ross-Trevor is adamant that the British one doesn't: "I don't think we could have done it, because the guitar stack was so loud you wouldn't have even heard the vocal. You'd have just picked up the guitar on the vocal mike."

It quickly became apparent to Ross-Trevor that the talent he was working with was a very special one indeed: "You can't help being just totally overawed by Hendrix. He was like nobody back then. He was the first person you ever saw to play that way." Yet Ross-Trevor didn't believe that Hendrix was even making the same kind of music as the kind of artist with whom he was used to working: "I didn't think of him in terms of pop. I remember thinking, 'This is more of an album band.' Really, nothing kind of stuck out as being, 'Oh this could be a number one.'" Indeed, Ross-Trevor didn't even realize at first that the tracks he was recording would feature vocals. "I actually didn't think he was a singer at all, on the first day," he reveals. "I just thought he was a guitarist, because the guitar was such a feature. Later in the evening when Chas said, 'Well, let's do some vocals,' it kind of surprised me a bit. I thought, 'Well—where are they gonna go?' Which is why I didn't think it was a singles band. To me, this was a jazz album."

Hendrix pulled the words to the songs from his back pocket (Ross-Trevor: "He'd written them all out on scruffy pieces of paper"), put on some headphones, and proceeded to undergo a strange transformation. So confident on the basic tracks when his guitar could do the talking for him, he became hesitant and insecure now that it was time to add his voice. "Chas had to work with him," says Ross-Trevor. "I remember it being long and drawn out. It wasn't a quick thing, whereas when he played the guitar it was like instant sound and instant performance and it was fantastic. When it came to the vocals, it did go on a bit and we did a lot of punching in—line by line, that kind of thing."

On December 14, 1966, a planned band practice was scrapped. The following day, Mitch Mitchell failed to turn up for either a recording session at CBS or a rehearsal, although some work was done at the studio. "Jimi and I messed around," reads Redding's diary entry for the day. This could be a reference to two untitled instrumental demos recorded at this session, which have yet to see the light of day. Rough mixes of "Foxy Lady," "3rd Stone from the Sun," and "Can You See Me" were also worked on. It is thought that more overdubbing work on "Hey Joe" was attempted at CBS, and this would have been the logical day for it to have been done. Ross-Trevor says, "I do remember trying an overdub on a De Lane Lea tape. It was for a guitar part, but I can't remember if the track was 'Hey Joe.' It could have been because the track was without vocal, so all I heard was an unknown backing track."

Asked whether he considered the mixes he worked on to be rough or master quality, Ross-Trevor shrugs: "Hard to tell, because back then you didn't spend two or three days mixing a track. Mixing didn't take that long—you only had four tracks. Mixing was only like 20 minutes, half an hour." One thing he is certain of is that the mixes were monaural: "Back then, all the sessions, you concentrated everything for the mono. The mono was king. All the effort went into the mono in every way. When it came to the stereo, it was like, 'Okay, I suppose we better do a stereo' and the attitude was, 'Well it's just stereo, who's got stereo?' It was mixed properly, but all the infinite little detailed things got forgotten in stereo."

His first two days of working with the Experience left Ross-Trevor elated. "Whether it was the sound I'd got or the sound they got, but I remember being really chuffed. I'd never recorded anything up to that point that sounded that good, so I remember going home on a high thinking, 'Wow, this is great.'"

Mitchell, it would seem, was less elated about the state of things. Though he might have been expected to be excited at being in a band that was just about to release its first single and had recorded an appearance on the most well-regarded pop program on television, Redding says that Mitchell's no-show on this day was somewhat typical of his attitude: "Chas did say on camera somewhere that every week we'd be looking for another drummer. Basically, [we were] not really getting on well with him. He used to be late all the time and didn't turn up. When times were tight, recording, Mitchell was always late." Etchingham adds, "Mitch Mitchell has a cavalier attitude to everything in life. He has a superiority complex which gives him that kind of persona: 'I'm the great Almighty.'"

It was this attitude which, around this time, led Hendrix to decide to audition another drummer with a view to firing Mitchell. Redding suggested John Banks, who had been a member of the recently disbanded Merseybeats and was then in a duo with Johnny Gustafson called John and Johnny. "Very good friend of mine," explains Redding. However, it was Banks's proficiency rather than sentimentality that ensured he made an impression at the audition. "Hendrix loved him," says Redding. "He fitted in well because he was a powerful type drummer. He wasn't as flamboyant as Mitchell, but he fitted in well with what we were doing. Hendrix said, 'Yeah, he's bloody good.' I said, 'I told you he's good.'" They decided to make the arrangement permanent. Redding: "We said to him, 'Do you want to do the job?' He said he hates flying." So ended the plan to oust Mitchell.

It was probably just as well. Whatever their misgivings about his personality and his punctuality, Mitchell's brilliance would be an integral reason for the artistic triumph of *Are You Experienced*. Redding does add that Mitchell's behavior eventually improved: "Chandler at some point docked him his wages for that week, and he was never late again."

the first single

ON DECEMBER 16, "HEY JOE" was released in the United Kingdom. Though it was a Track Records release, it sported a Polydor label. "The artwork wasn't ready for Track, for the printing, and we just wanted to get it out," explains Stamp. "We said, 'Okay, stick Polydor on, that's fine.'" For Stamp, the single was a stepping stone rather than something particularly significant in itself. "If you look at 'Hey Joe' in the context of the time it was released, that wasn't a guaranteed hit record at all," he says. "I liked it as a record. My first thoughts were, 'It's not an obvious commercial single,' but it didn't matter because this whole idea was gonna move on. We had ideas and plans to try this for at least six months. Sometimes the first singles aren't immediate hits. But I thought it contained the essence of that guitar sound that we all think of as Jimi. You heard that. That touched you."

Although conventional material both brilliant ("You Keep Me Hangin' On" by the Supremes) and lightweight ("What Would I Be" by rocking-chaired crooner Val Doonican) was currently riding high in the British charts, "Hey Joe"'s air of sophistication would not have come as a complete culture shock for radio listeners. Also doing well in the hit parade at that juncture was "Dead End Street," the darkest of the Kinks' many class-conscious songs, and "My Mind's Eye," in which the Small Faces befuddled a lot of their teenybopper fans with their take on the drone and quasi-mysticism of the voguish psychedelia. Perhaps it was these increasing signs of musical development that led to a favorable critical reception to "Hey Joe." Certainly, rock criticism at the time was not renowned for its perception: it was only the previous year that some writers had dismissed Bob Dylan's cataclysmically brilliant "Like a Rolling Stone" as unlistenable. Derek Johnson of the *New Musical Express* described "Hey Joe" as a "Raw, uninhibited treatment of a traditional number" and was particularly taken by its "insidious r 'n' b pattern . . . thundering drums . . . spine-tingling guitar work and . . . hypnotic slow beat." He concluded that "This is a disc for the connoisseurs." Peter Jones of *Record Mirror* declared that it was a "slow burner of immense excitement" and said that if justice prevailed it would be "a first time hit." Although the positive reviews of "Hey Joe" didn't appear in print before Christmas, they were an encouraging start to the band's career.

Jones added in his review, "Flip is more urgent and equally soul-laden." He was, of course, speaking about the record's B-side, "Stone Free." For many, this song exemplifies one of the most extraordinary aspects of Hendrix's career; that he could produce a song of this quality in what was considered his debut writing venture is only just short of miraculous. Leaving aside the fact that it wasn't really the debut composition it was long believed to be, "Stone Free" is an inordinately confident and powerful early accomplishment. Hendrix expounds a belief in personal freedom to a jaw-socking musical backing containing a fearsomely loud guitar solo.

However, this author remains unconvinced that the song is quite as good as its admirers make out. First, it is just a bit too sonically brutal to be completely enjoyable. That musical failing is compounded by shortcomings in the lyric. In 1966, the hostility expressed by many rock artists toward the concept of marriage was understandable considering its connections to censorial orthodox religion and its connotations of being trapped in an unhappy union in a society where divorce was very rare. Yet artists frequently confused that stance with an antipathy toward women (the Rolling Stones being the most notorious culprits). Of course, it would be absurd to take umbrage at everything that smacks of what one would now call political incorrectness—not least because modern "girlie" culture seems no less unpleasant and hypocritical than old macho culture—but one gets the uncomfortable feeling from some lines in "Stone Free" that Hendrix is inviting us to applaud not just his free spirit, but a love 'em and leave 'em attitude. Nonetheless, "Stone Free" is an important statement: it was a piece of work that was utterly uncompromising, geared toward no one's agenda but the author's. Writing-wise, this was exactly as Hendrix meant to continue.

December 16 was also the date on which the Experience's *Ready, Steady, Go!* performance of "Hey Joe" was broadcast. Unfortunately, no recording is known to survive of the performance (which, like all British TV then, was shown in black and white). Also on the 16th, the Experience played a gig at Chislehurst Caves.

On December 21, Chandler returned to CBS Studios but, contrary to some reports, not with the Experience, and not to work on a song called "First Look Around the Corner." Little is known about this track, as it has yet to surface even on bootleg. Chances are, in any case, that the song—mentioned by Hendrix in a contemporaneous interview—was not a new song, but probably a working title for one of the tracks that ended up on *Are You Experienced*. In fact, the Experience would never record at CBS again, due to a falling out between Chandler and studio manager Jacques Levy. "After the first block of recordings, Chas wanted to book more recording time but Levy would only let him book time if his bill up to that point was settled, and he also asked for payment upfront for any future recording," recalls Mike Ross. "Chas lost his temper and said, 'This is not the way I do business, I've never been treated like this before in any other studio. I normally come in, do the sessions and I normally pay later when the invoices come in.' But the studio manager didn't know who he was—wasn't a company or anything, didn't have any security that he could put up."

Subsequent to the row, Chandler tried to obtain the recordings the band had made at CBS so that they could be worked on at other studios. Understandably, Levy refused to hand them over until Chandler coughed up the money. Chandler eventually did so, and his visit on the 21st was to collect the tapes, which Levy, after walking across from his office on the opposite side of New Bond Street, instructed Ross-Trevor to release to him. Chandler remonstrated to Levy about his treatment, but Levy was uninterested and shortly left. Chandler sat talking for a while with Ross-Trevor and made his unhappiness clear. "He was just going on and on about it," says Ross-Trevor. "He just wouldn't let it go. 'It's such a shame,' he said. 'I'm really happy with the sound here. I'm really pleased with what we've got.' And he actually said, 'We've got better results here than at De Lane Lea and it's a real shame we can't continue the album.'" Ross-Trevor, though, perceived a financial dilemma beneath the genuine anger: "Obviously he didn't have any money because if he was that knocked out with the studio, he would have put his own money in. He would have carried on and paid the bill. But he was obviously hoping to make the album and then get an advance from a record company to pay the bills."

Such were the pathetic hand-to-mouth circumstances Chandler and his charges were living through as they attempted to put together an album that would go down as one of the greatest ever recorded. As if to illustrate this, that night they played a gig at Blaises to keep the money dribbling in.

Though Ross-Trevor went on to become one of the biggest names in his field, working with luminaries including Fleetwood Mac, Brian Auger, Cat Stevens, and the Byrds (he now works as an orchestral engineer on film scoring sessions), he still holds a fond place in his heart for the mysterious and gifted guitarist whose rapid exit from his professional life was "a major disappointment to me, because I really enjoyed the sessions. I loved them and wanted to carry on. I knew it was special. I knew this could do me some good as an engineer." Following Hendrix to his next port of call wasn't an option: "In those days, there wasn't such a thing as freelance engineers. Engineers were tied to studios."

On December 22, the Experience played two shows at the Guildhall in the coastal town of Southampton, supporting Geno Washington and the Ram Jam Band. Christmas 1966 saw everybody involved with the Jimi Hendrix Experience, except Hendrix and Etchingham, off to spend the festive period with their families. With Etchingham estranged from her own family and Hendrix far away from his, the two spent a quiet day in the flat in Montagu Square. On December 26—

Boxing Day in Britain—it was back to business, with the Experience playing a gig at the Upper Cut in Forest Gate, London. While waiting for the band to go on, Chandler noticed Hendrix playing an interesting riff in the dressing room. He'd actually first heard it at the flat about ten days before and had remarked on how much he liked it then. Now he told Hendrix to construct a song around it. "I remember the day," says Redding. "Some boxer owned this club. Hendrix basically got the riff going before we played, and then we did our gig and I think he went home, wrote it and that was our second single." Thus was born "Purple Haze," the song that would illustrate to the public that "Hey Joe" was just the first wave of the ocean that was Hendrix's genius.

The lyric that Hendrix devised for the track was as inspired as the riff was unforgettable and the melody resplendent. It did go through a transformation, however—possibly a few—before it became the lyric familiar to millions. "'Purple Haze' originated from a visit to Hyde Park Corner—Speakers' Corner—where somebody had a placard saying 'Jesus Saves,'" says Etchingham. "And he actually wrote that. He actually started the lyrics with 'Purple Haze/Jesus Saves.' That's part of where it came from."

A handwritten draft of this original lyric, inspired by the characters who declaim their beliefs from orange crates at that famous haunt of London's eccentrics, can be seen in the booklet that accompanies the 1997 CD reissue of *Are You Experienced*. Though the lyric offers an image of "1,000 crosses," it would seem that even at this stage the words were actually a conflation of inspiration provided both by the Speaker's Corner characters and by a science fiction story

Hendrix had read. Hendrix told journalist Keith Altham, "It was just a straight dream I had linked upon a story I read in a science fiction magazine about a purple death ray." The story Hendrix refers to is almost certainly *Night of Light*, by Philip José Farmer. Said story uses the phrase "purple haze" at least once to describe the disorienting and dizzying visual effects of sunspot activity on a planet called Dante's Joy. Though *Night of Light* was published as a novel in June 1966, a shorter version of it had been published in a magazine called *Fantasy & Science Fiction* in June 1957. The spine of an edition of that magazine is visible in a photograph of Hendrix that appears in the booklet of the CD *South Saturn Delta*: Hendrix is hunched over a stereo, beneath which is a shelf of books and magazines. Though the picture is cropped in such a way as to make it unclear whether it is the June 1957 edition of that magazine, the evidence does seem to stack up in favor of the Farmer story being the source of Hendrix's song.

Farmer explains of his story, "It's part of what became the Father John Carmody series about an interstellar Roman Catholic priest. This is before he became a priest, and he was a wife murderer fleeing interstellar justice. He went to this one particular planet called Dante's Joy, which had some very curious things going on at regular intervals. The star exerted influence on the planet and they changed their forms more or less to conform to the particular type of individual they were." Those inhabitants of Dante's Joy who choose not to hibernate through these periods of solar upheaval experience a form of madness which leads them to harm others, something that fits in with Hendrix's lyric about "acting funny but I don't know why" (though he attributes his confusion to a female partner). Farmer himself has never heard "Purple Haze," partly as a result of not being a rock consumer, and remained completely unaware that his work had inspired an all-time rock classic until the late 1990s: "I'm always the last to know. I didn't know anything about it until a granddaughter of mine picked it up on the network [Internet] and she sent me something about it." He was tickled by the idea of the song when he heard about it. "I'm always pleased if I inspire somebody else to do something. And I understand he was high in the rock groups' regard."

Redding, incidentally, points out the fallacy of those who assume the lyric is the transcription of an acid trip: "He hadn't taken LSD then." Redding says that Hendrix's stimulants at this time were merely "a few pints of bitter and a reefer."

On December 29, the Experience performed "Hey Joe" live on the BBC TV chart program *Top of the Pops* with the Breakaways. On New Year's Eve 1966, the Experience performed at the Hillside Social Club, in Folkestone, Kent. Redding had secured this booking due to being a local boy. "A place I used to play," he says. "We got fifty quid for it." Etchingham points out that gigs in such unglamorous venues were in no way uncommon at this stage of the Experience's career: "They were terrible. Like, working men's clubs. Almost spit and sawdust. They were poky little clubs."

Following the gig, Mitchell returned to London, but the rest of the party stayed behind. "Hendrix, Kathy, and me and our road manager drove down to my mum's house and we got there and we had a glass of something for the New Year," recalls Redding. It was while billeted here that Hendrix got

the idea for one of the most powerful tracks on *Are You Experienced*. Redding: "He wandered in and it was cold—and he still wasn't used to the English cold—and he met me mum and he said, 'Can I stand next to your fire?' She said, 'Of course.'" Redding points out that it wasn't merely the theme and lyrical refrain of the song "Fire" that Hendrix acquired on this evening, but also the phrase he calls out before going into his guitar solo on the track: "There was a dog there and he said, 'Move over, Rover.' We had a couple of drinks and stayed the night there and went back up to town the next day. I don't think he wrote the lyric that night, but that gave him the idea."

The Experience's first gig of 1967 was on January 4. More gigs followed the next week, at one of which (in Sheffield) they were charmingly billed as "The New Weirdo Trio Experience Jimi Hendrick's [sic] Experience."

Meanwhile, "Hey Joe" was making its first appearances on the U.K. charts. At that point there was no definitive pop chart in Britain. Music papers *New Musical Express, Melody Maker, Record Mirror*, and *Disc* commissioned and published their own chart listings. The *New Musical Express's* chart was considered slightly more authoritative than the others simply because the music paper boasted the largest circulation and had been the first to publish a chart. Although the *Guinness Book of British Hit Singles* now seeks to give the impression of inviolable chart positions for that period, that there was no such thing is illustrated by the fact that it has the Beatles' "Please Please Me" climbing only to number two, whereas most charts at the time—and the general popular impression, including that of the Beatles—was that it was the first Fab

Four number one hit. The BBC decided which acts to book on *Top of the Pops*—its TV chart show—by using an aggregate of the figures in all of the various charts. When, in 1969, the BBC began using the chart compiled by the British Market Research Bureau for *Record Retailer* (later retitled *Music Week*), the U.K. equivalent of *Billboard*, this chart began to be perceived as the authoritative one.

In the second week of January, the frequent storminess of the relationship between Hendrix and Etchingham spilled over into a furious, ear-splitting row which, ironically, gave rise to one of Hendrix's most tender and affecting lyrics. Hendrix had complained to Etchingham, not for the first time, that her cooking was terrible. Etchingham picked up his plate of food and smashed it on the floor. When Hendrix loudly took umbrage at this, Etchingham picked up some more plates and proceeded to throw them at the walls. Their deafening argument culminated in Etchingham storming out, with Hendrix following close behind. Etchingham eluded Hendrix by catching a cab and spent the night at the home of Eric Burdon, with whom her ex-flatmate Angela King was now living. She returned to Montagu Square the next day. Asked if Hendrix was apologetic, she replies, "Sheepish, is the right word. Not apologetic. Jimi was never very apologetic about anything. We were all right. It was just one of those rows that you have and then you start talking to each other again. After a couple of days of cold shoulder."

Though Hendrix wasn't apologetic in the conventional sense, in her absence he had written a quite beautiful song—a lyric without a melody—about Etchingham and their argument that could be considered a form of an apology. The

Above *An early shot of Hendrix with Curtis Knight and the Squires. He would never be this clean-cut again.*

Left *An early publicity shot, taken in central London's Marylebone area. Hendrix's home in Montagu Square is literally around the corner.*

Right *As he rose to fame, Hendrix cultivated his look as well as his music.*

Left *Hendrix at home, displaying the influence upon him of other sixties icons, Lenny Bruce and Bob Dylan.*

Right *Jimi Hendrix at the Monterey Festival, June 1967. The event made his reputation in the United States.*

Above *The other two thirds of the Jimi Hendrix Experience: Dependable bassist Noel Redding (left) and blazing drummer Mitch Mitchell (right).*

Above *A familiar huddle: Hendrix conferring with Chas Chandler, manager and mentor.*

Above *Despite the matching afros, it was apparent from the beginning who would be the center of attention.*

Left *With Eric Clapton, who was also known as "God"—that is, until Hendrix's arrival on the scene.*

Right *Hendrix's extraordinary live shows soon made him an integral part of the music royalty of Swinging London.*

Above *With a host of musical luminaries including Roy Wood of the Move and Syd Barrett.*

Above *Hendrix posing with the Who.*

Above *Hendrix cuts a lone figure in the studio. Note (left) the elongated thumb that allowed him to play so many of his unique chords.*

Above *Performing at the Marquee, London, for the German TV show* Beat Club.

Above *Time behind the mixing desk was as important for Hendrix as time in front of a microphone or audience.*

Above *Even in the pub, Hendrix looked larger than life.*

Left *Betweeen the constant touring and recording, there was still time for moments of playfulness.*

Right *Hendrix also played guitar with his teeth. Or did he? Some thought it was merely grandstanding.*

Above *Sadder times: A stimulant-addled Hendrix is escorted from a wrecked Swedish hotel room in 1968.*

James Marshall Hendrix, 1942–1970

song was "The Wind Cries Mary." Its lyric speaks of footprints dressed in red, traffic lights turning blue, and small hours when jacks are back in their boxes. All of this relates specifically to the pair's falling out. Etchingham was wearing a red dress that night. In addition, "The traffic lights were there," says Etchingham. "Of course they didn't turn blue—they turn red, but it doesn't rhyme. And 'all the jacks' means when the television finished in those days, because there was the little girl with the jack in the box which indicated the television was finished for the night. It was a test card that they used to put on at the end of the programs when they were closing down."

Despite being the subject of a song that is now regarded as a classic by millions, Etchingham reveals that she was not overwhelmed by "The Wind Cries Mary." "I was never very impressed by any of them. I really wasn't that interested in that side of things. I know that there are people who are intensely interested in their partner's work and music and everything, but I wasn't like that. And in fact if they were having a conversation about music and they were all sitting in the sitting room, me and Lotta used to go out shopping or go and visit a friend. Or go to the hairdresser's. Do the things that girls do. We didn't sit there hanging on every word. We didn't know what we were seeing. We didn't know a legend was developing in front of us. We just knew he was good." Even today, Etchingham isn't inclined to savor her footnote in rock history: "I really don't listen to Jimi's music. I don't dwell on the past. If it comes up on the radio, fair enough but I don't go out of my way to carry on playing his stuff."

Hendrix once claimed that "The Wind Cries Mary" was "not about any one person." What would have seemed to be a disingenuous or diplomatic quote is cast in a new light by a claim by ex-girlfriend Mary Washington, aka Regina, that in 1966 he had already written its title and its most beautiful couplet—"Somewhere a Queen is weeping/Somewhere a King has no wife"—as part of a poem of no more than six lines. "I remember these writings on a piece of paper," she told *Univibes* magazine. "And I asked him about it. 'Why are you writing a song about Mary?' And he said, 'I am not writing the song per se about a woman named Mary. The song is about us.' So, I said, 'If the song is about us, why didn't you write like Regina, with my name?' He said, 'You know, I don't know anybody named Mary, but your name does mean Queen.'" This suggests that the song was half formed in Hendrix's mind already and that the row with Etchingham merely spurred him to finish it. (It would appear to be simple coincidence that Mary was Etchingham's middle name.)

"The Wind Cries Mary" was one of four tracks on which the Experience worked on January 11, 1967, this time back at De Lane Lea. The other songs recorded on this date were the basic track of "Purple Haze," a new basic track for "3rd Stone from the Sun" and "51st Anniversary." Redding observes of the latter track's multiple overdubs, "That's when all the old experimenting started to come in. Chandler was well into that and Jimi was well into that." Chandler would say of the song, "It was the first time where we consciously thought of approaching production that way. There were five guitar overdubs in all, linking in together to sound like one guitar."

"51st Anniversary" was—amazingly—recorded, over-dubbed, and completed that day. That the band could master a song they'd never heard before from beginning to end in a recording session at which they recorded three other songs, and furthermore, that this song turned out to be fabulous, displays that this was a band who was simply on fire creatively, and the outtakes from that session that have leaked out confirm it. Early takes break down quickly, but the band rapidly get to grips with the number. This leaves Hendrix free to add guitar overdubs and vocals. One thankfully rejected mix has Hendrix's voice recorded twice and then put completely out of synch to create an effect that is more duet than double track. This mix finishes with a much longer bout of guitar wail than is heard on the familiar version's close, which ends abruptly and is followed by coughing and Hendrix mumbling something about a verse.

The Experience restarted "3rd Stone from the Sun" from scratch rather than use anything from the demo recorded at CBS. Several takes were attempted before a satisfactory basic track was achieved. This basic track would ultimately become little more than hazy background to the myriad vocal and guitar effects that Hendrix would add at a later date.

The work they'd planned for the day was completed, but there was still some time left on the session that would have to be paid for even if the band sat around doing nothing. Though Chandler might have been happy to experiment on "51st Anniversary," he was still cost conscious. "We had twenty minutes left or something and Chas said to Jimi, 'Have you got anything else?'" remembers Redding. As it transpired, Hendrix did have something: the song he had written for

Etchingham after their row, which he had now set to a melody. "Hendrix taught me the thing and we recorded it," says Redding. "We put down 'The Wind Cries Mary' in twenty minutes. We'd never rehearsed it or nothing." During that twenty minutes, Hendrix also added guitar overdubs. Though this recording was probably intended as a demo—and though an attempt was made to rerecord it at a later session—such was the professionalism of the result this day that this take of "The Wind Cries Mary" was the one that would be used for the Jimi Hendrix Experience's third single.

Amazingly, the band had significant live commitments to fulfill the same day, and performed two shows at the Bag O' Nails. This would be the pattern of the recording of *Are You Experienced*. Yet this hard workload was something that did not bother the group. "I liked the way we did it," says Redding. "We'd go and do a club, we'd work until nine-ish and then in those days it's only forty-five minute sets and we'd be in the studio by about eleven and we'd work for a couple of hours and we'd go home to bed. Doing a gig and then going in a studio, you're all set up." He does add, though, "We were all very young and keen."

The Bag O' Nails gig turned out to be very important for Hendrix because it was at this concert that he met Roger Mayer, a man who would become as important to Hendrix's sound as Marshall amplifiers. Mayer was helping to revolutionize the sound of the electric guitar with gadgets and devices he was inventing and supplying to guitar-playing friends such as Jeff Beck and Jimmy Page, with whom he'd grown up. It's possible that Hendrix was aware of Mayer before this gig, because Mayer knew the former members of the original Animals well. "'Hey Joe' had been released, and I met Jimi and spoke to him and sort of told him about some of the sounds I was into and was experimenting with," recalls Mayer. "He suggested I come down to a gig in a short while at Chislehurst Caves."

With the exception of the 13th, the band played gigs in various parts of the United Kingdom January 12–16, one of which saw them sharing the bill with future reggae superstar Jimmy Cliff. The "poky" venues, as Etchingham describes them, were rapidly becoming less appropriate for a band of the Experience's stature. By now "Hey Joe" was number 11 in one chart. The Experience was going places, and it was perhaps this fact that gave then enough courage to request a pay rise at this juncture. The management agreed to £25 per week, an almost doublefold increase.

According to Mitchell, on January 17 the Experience, unsatisfied with the first version of ". . . Mary," recorded another version, again at De Lane Lea, which was ultimately not used. That this session took place cannot be verified, although ". . . Mary" certainly was recorded again, probably on February 3, although this would be at Olympic, not De Lane Lea. A couple of things the Experience certainly did do on January 17 was record a (never aired) session for Radio Luxembourg (whose beamed-in broadcasts to a Britain with literally no commercial pop radio were hugely important in promoting records and acts) and play another show at the 7½ Club in London.

The *Top of the Pops* audience was treated to another performance of "Hey Joe" on January 18, 1967, the same day as the audience at the 7½ Club was treated to another show by the Experience. Still spurning—or perhaps unable to afford—studio work, the band concentrated on live performances for the rest of the month and beyond. One of the more special gigs took place on January 24 at the Marquee in London, where the Experience not only broke the house attendance record, but also played to an audience that included all four Beatles, more than one member of the Rolling Stones, Eric Clapton, and Jeff Beck. It was back to a more mundane live setting on January 25 when the Experience played the Orford Cellar in rustic Norwich. On January 20, Hendrix was granted his longest work permit thus far, this one for a period of six months.

On January 27, at the Experience's second gig at Chislehurst Caves, Hendrix hooked up once more with sound experimenter Roger Mayer, who gave him some gizmos to vary the sound of his guitar. "I showed him the Octavia, which was one of my new inventions," says Mayer, "and another form of distortion, fuzzbox. These were entirely experimental—development models." It would be the start of a personal friendship, and of a professional relationship that saw Mayer working exclusively with the American.

Mayer was actually a guitarist himself, but had spurned the professional path chosen by his childhood friends Page and Beck. "I was a bit more interested in the technical sound, into the sound side, and not particularly into traveling around and playing in pubs and that," he explains. Instead, he moved into a rather posh job: "I was working with the Royal Naval Scientific Service, which is the scientific branch of the Admiralty. I ended up there as an assistant experiential officer, working at the Admiralty research laboratory in

Teddington. We were involved with vibrational and acoustical analysis, to do with making boats quieter and listening to noises, all generally to do with underwater warfare, which is what the Navy's all about, really. Working with hydrophones, microphones, all sorts of sound analysis equipment." His rock 'n' roll experiments—although working on the same acoustical principles—were very much a contrast to this prim and proper day job: "I'd been involved with making some early fuzzboxes that were used back in 1964 on a couple of number one records by P. J. Proby. 'Hold Me' and 'Together'—that was probably the first Number One record in England there had been using a fuzzbox." There were also quite a few records on which Mayer's invention was used that he will probably never know about: "I never paid that much attention to it. Jimmy Page was very prolific then on an awful lot of pop records. He was playing for virtually everybody."

On January 29 the Experience played probably their most prestigious gig to date—other than the Paris Olympia—when they appeared at the Saville Theatre in London's Shaftesbury Avenue. The Saville had become a venue for upmarket rock concerts since Brian Epstein had decided to rent the building—which, like other theatres in the West End, was closed on the Sabbath—in order to stage special Sunday musical events. On this particular day, the Experience were bottom of the bill to the Who, the Koobas, and the Thoughts. Hendrix thrived in the unusually plush conditions and turned in a performance that made converts of yet more members of the pop aristocracy. Although Eric Clapton had already been alerted to the fact that the rock world had a genius on its hands, it was at this gig that both

Pete Townshend and Jack Bruce experienced a Road to Damascus conversion. Townshend was so shell-shocked that, following Hendrix on stage with the Who, he found himself incapable of his usual arm windmilling and extroversion. Bruce, meanwhile, as well as lamenting that the Experience had stolen all of Cream's intended thunder in the subsequent rag-chewing at Brian Epstein's flat (see the Forming the Experience chapter), went off and wrote the riff of what would become "Sunshine of Your Love" specifically as a tribute to Hendrix. The finished song would become Cream's first U.S. Top Ten single. Ironically, when Cream disbanded, it was this song that Hendrix decided to play as an impromptu tribute to them in the famous 1969 live broadcast (and floor-manager-traumatizing) *A Happening for Lulu* show, abandoning the agreed-upon performance of "Hey Joe."

The Experience returned to the Saville Theatre on January 31 to shoot a promotional film for "Hey Joe." On January 30 the Experience did a session for the BBC Light program *Pop North* at Broadcasting House in London. Unfortunately, none of the three tracks recorded on this particular date—"Hey Joe," "Rock Me Baby," and "Foxy Lady"— survived to make it onto the 1998 CD *BBC Sessions*.

the Olympic sessions

THE FIRST DAY OF FEBRUARY 1967 saw the Experience play the New Cellar Club in South Shields, near Newcastle-Upon-Tyne. It was while here on his home turf that Chandler phoned London and found out that "Hey Joe" had leapt to Number 7 on one of the charts.

After a performance in Darlington the following day, the band returned south, played at the Ricky Tick Club in Hounslow on February 3, and had another recording session scheduled for that same day. This one was to be the first at Olympic Studios, by far the best studio the Experience had yet worked in. Unfortunately, the Ricky Tick Club had been the scene of yet another destructive stage act by Hendrix. "Hendrix put his guitar into the ceiling and wrecked it," remembers Redding. Hendrix was left without an instrument for possibly the band's most important recording session so far. A mate of Redding's came to the rescue: "I had to make a phone call to an old friend of mine from Folkestone, and someone sent a taxi and Hendrix played my Telecaster backwards."

Olympic, located in the sleepy London suburb of Barnes, was another of the then rare (but increasingly common) independent studios. Olympic Studios had been set up in the early sixties at its original site on Carlton Street in London. It relocated to a former cinema in Barnes in 1966. The new Olympic was on the first floor of its building and, though it was a single recording room, with measurements of 60 feet by 40 feet by 28 feet, it was massively larger than the previous places the Experience had recorded in. Olympic had state-of-the-art equipment. It also had an ergonomic mixing desk, created in-house, largely by Dick Sweatenham (later of Helios Electronics) and the studio manager Keith Grant. Grant had worked out which buttons he hit most often during a session and designed the mixing desk accordingly. The "wraparound" design of the desk enabled the engineer to reach the furthest knobs on both of its ends simultaneously. This was extraordinary—even unique at the time—for a desk of such complexity, and made it very easy for engineers to avoid making mistakes.

Olympic's third distinctive attribute was its informality. Though it had been designed for recording MOR music, advertisements, and film soundtracks, and though Keith Grant was not particularly enamored of rock 'n' roll, the studio prided itself on being inventive and efficient, and its young staff were the kind of people rock musicians felt comfortable around. George Chkiantz—who, as a 23-year-old new to the business, worked as a tape op on the Olympic *Are You Experienced* tracks and graduated to an engineering role on the Experience's second album—recalls the ambience of the studio: "The kind of engineers that we were at Olympic I took for granted, but we were very unusual. Engineers in the more conventional studios wore white coats, didn't talk to the clients, would only interface through the producer. The client didn't come into the control room. We broke a lot of rules." No rock band of the time was more comfortable with such unconventional attitudes than the Rolling Stones, Olympic's major rock clients. Chkiantz: "Because the Stones were recording at Olympic, Olympic was very much a name to conjure with. We did a lot of work." Hendrix had actually visited Olympic the previous November to watch the Rolling Stones record "Ruby Tuesday." That was probably his first visit to the studio.

Hendrix's own first Olympic session marked the start of his professional relationship with South African-born Eddie Kramer. Although Kramer does not seem to have had a friendship with him outside the studio, he was clearly considered valuable by the guitarist: he was to become Hendrix's permanent engineer. In addition to Kramer's technical knowledge, there could also have been another reason for Hendrix's comfort with Kramer. British engineers (indeed, anybody working in Britain at that time) were, as a rule, not very service oriented, but as Vic Briggs, who worked with Kramer in the new Animals, points out: "He kind of embarrassed me, because I was not used to this: 'How can I help you? How can I help you get what *you* want? I'm here to serve you.' It was an attitude that I really hadn't encountered, being brought up in England."

Both Etchingham and Stamp, however, don't feel any one individual could, or did, make much difference in how Hendrix operated when recording, due to his extraordinary ability to pick things up with incredible speed. Stamp: "It became apparent . . . that he understood the studio. He picked up the whole idea of recording just as quickly. People talk about, 'Oh, Jimi played that song for the first time. He'd never ever played it before. He heard it for the first time and he played it.' Which is the flavor of genius. I'm not saying that Jimi was a genius, but he certainly had that flavor. That was how it was in the studio. He knew more about recording than Eddie Kramer after a couple of hours. The gift was that he was with Eddie Kramer, so he learned from a great master."

"It wouldn't have mattered who the engineer was," says Etchingham. "It just happened that he was there. Jimi was a maestro. He could hear the music in his mind. He knew exactly what sound he wanted. He was able to direct his own music entirely. He'd been in recording studios before. He knew the score. Chas was mainly in charge, but Chas said that Jimi's input was enormous—and that's when he started to realize that Jimi wasn't just going to be instructed in what to do. Maybe Eddie Kramer said, 'If you push this button, you'll get this sound,' but that would register in Jimi's mind and then he would shout: 'Push that further. Let's have more treble on that.' He was giving the instructions."

George Chkiantz, however, has no doubt as to the importance of Kramer to the Experience: "It's really easy to take the piss out of Eddie," he acknowledges. "He's very ambitious and precious." Yet he adds of Kramer's work with Hendrix, "He had to be able to get his head 'round what it was that was out there in order to get it down on the tape. Not just anybody could have done that. If they weren't able to encompass it, get it into the field of what they could grasp, they would have narrowed it and diminished it and taken the power away. A lot of the engineers at the time would have, and to my pretty certain knowledge did, absolutely hate the racket that Hendrix was making. The cutting engineers hated it. Didn't want to know. It was so distorted and so problematic. Now it's amazing how normal it seems, but you cannot imagine the way people would just put their hands over their ears and run away screaming. I think that a lot of credit on that has got to go to Eddie. He's quite keen on very avant-garde jazz—I often wondered whether that was a fashion statement—but, for whatever reason, that sort of put him as a person who was quite prepared and quite used to listening to stuff that wasn't within the rules. Certainly I think that he was the right person for the job." He also points out that Hendrix must have felt the same way: "Subsequently loads of [engineers] wanted to get their mitts on Hendrix and it didn't happen really, did it?"

The Olympic sessions saw the Experience being recorded in a manner that was a marked contrast to the methods employed at the CBS sessions, where Hendrix had used microphones placed at a distance of twelve feet. "They were close-mike sessions," recalls Chkiantz. "We may well have taken direct feeds as well as the mikes, as and when occasion decided. Eddie would sit and twiddle with the EQ for a long, long, long time in discussion with Hendrix. He'd have mixtures of close miking and distance miking. I thought Eddie close-miked more than was reasonable, but then he'd use a certain amount of compression, using a device to squash the dynamics of the sound." Kramer was not afraid to place delicate equipment in the path of the sonic blast of the Experience: "As well as the usual mikes, Eddie used a very nice ribbon mike quite extensively. He used Beyer M160s. He used them a lot on Noel, Hendrix. They're quite delicate, but they produce a very nice sound. It would be unusual to use them in these sort of circumstances. I think we must have been repairing [them] at a fair old rate."

Another change to Hendrix's recording technique that took place at Olympic was the result of an audacious idea on the part of Kramer. He made the decision to use all four tracks for the "basic": rhythm guitar on one track, bass on a second, and drums on the remaining two. Previously, at least one track would have been left free for adding vocals or other instruments, but Kramer was using up the first generation of tape before the overdubbing stage. Vocals, guitar solos, sound effects, backing vocals, etc., would then be added on the "bounce down," the process whereby—in an age of four-track recording—space was made for more instruments and sounds on tape by reducing, for example, the four tracks of the first tape generation to two tracks on the next tape generation, leaving two tracks free for further overdubs. The downside of this process was the inevitable deterioration of sound quality, with the deterioration increasing incrementally with each tape generation—hence the normal practice of getting as many overdubs on each generation as possible. Yet using up that first tape generation on the basic meant that Hendrix had a power in determining the overall sound that he had not had previously. Whereas a basic track with the whole drum kit squashed onto one track and guitar and bass squashed onto another made for limited room for maneuver if one element had to be mixed up or down—often one could not bring up the guitar without also bringing up the bass if they were on the same track—now Hendrix could mold the track as he liked. "Once they got the basic venture on tape, the mixdowns were therefore something that could be gone over, maybe different versions could be got," says Chkiantz, adding, "Although that didn't actually happen—when they settled for one, they normally settled for it."

It was an initiative that would not have been possible in some other studios. "Three generations were generally regarded as what you could get away with before tape hiss and wow and flutter were going to come up and bite you badly," explains Chkiantz. "However, at Olympic, our machines were actually very good and we reckoned we could get away with an extra generation, which was quite a major thing. Eddie used that so that he split the band very much more in the way you would have done it on eight- or sixteen-track. I wouldn't say it was an invention. A precursor, perhaps. People at the time wouldn't have claimed it as even a particularly good idea because it forced you through another generation on the drums, which were normally the most sensitive to copying losses. Eddie always thought he could EQ his way out of it—and the results are yours to hear." As the last comment indicates, Chkiantz had his doubts: "I don't actually think the generations added. I think the texture of the album would have been different, but I don't think it would have been worse [without it.] Some of the tracks by Dave Siddle and others are also very good, after all. On the whole, sadly, extra layers of noise, extra layers of machine deficiencies—wow and flutter, extra layers of EQ—are to your disadvantage. Guys like Eddie had to make decisions at a time when he didn't know what was coming next." Chkiantz recalls that the hand-to-mouth nature of Hendrix's lyric writing added to the problem: "It's one thing if you know what the song's going to be and you can hear in your head the vocal, but how the hell can you hear it in your head when the guy hasn't sung it yet, hasn't even written it yet? I certainly remember him writing down the lyrics and thinking them up. He may have had an idea of which direction they were going in [but] I doubt whether they were completed until the last moment."

Nevertheless, Hendrix was pleased with Kramer's initiative: "I think he—maybe egged on by Chas—felt it very important that Jimi and the band should have control over what the mixes were," says Chkiantz. All of this ensured, Chkiantz thinks, that Hendrix felt completely comfortable with his engineer: "Hendrix was convinced that Eddie understood him and was aiming for the same goals. That's very important for an artist of his type. Imagine how difficult it must be for an artist who's down there playing. He looks up into the control room and sees an engineer who clearly doesn't like what he's hearing and is just being polite about it. Where does he go from there? How does he judge whether he's done a good take or not?"

On this first Olympic session, the Experience stood, as they always would at this studio, facing the glass of the elevated control booth, the vastness of the remainder of the studio stretching behind them. They recorded the backing track for "Fire" (complete with guitar solo overdub), guitar and vocal overdubs on "Purple Haze," overdubs and mixing on "Foxy Lady," and a new basic track for "The Wind Cries Mary." In attendance was Roger Mayer, invited by Hendrix. Mayer's latest device, the Octavia, ensured that "Purple Haze," which already sounded special, was given an even greater air of surreality via a guitar solo distorted to sound like no guitar solo before. Mayer explains of his creation, "It's a foot pedal with circuitry in it that doubles the frequency of the sound you put in, but in so doing—because a guitar string has many overtones—when you actually start doubling all the overtones, the guitar almost takes on like a flute sound. The actual box is touch sensitive as well, so it does use some other tricks in the box to make it actually change depending upon how you play. It does produce a sound that is completely unique. It is sort of a natural sound, but it is an unnatural sound because the strings have some overtones that, when you double them and you combine them with another string, would become discordant or alien-sounding because they don't naturally occur. Once you apply a mathematical process to a sound, it does take it completely into a new dimension. The box is a little bit like putting two mirrors together and then putting an image in the middle: you get multiple images of it all."

Mayer was on hand to make sure Hendrix had no problems with this still-experimental gadget. "It was a brand new box and I would go out in the studio with Jimi, listen to the sounds, go back in the control room and listen to it, and then come back and see if there's any adjustments to be made and speak to Jimi about how it feels." Chandler was quite happy for this experimenting to be taking place. Important as he considered thrift, he appreciated that he had an artist on his hands who was blowing away all notions of what could be done in pop. "Chas and Jimi, once we heard the sounds, knew that this was groundbreaking stuff," says Mayer. "You've got to realize, then people had only heard 'Hey Joe' and very, very few people had seen him live by that time, so it was a completely revolutionary sound step for him." Mayer says that without the use of the Octavia, ". . . they wouldn't have sounded revolutionary. It wouldn't have begun Jimi's psychedelia. It wouldn't have taken it to that extreme."

The album would feature other gadgets of Mayer's, including Fuzzfaces—a type of Fuzzbox—specially modified by

Mayer for the guitarist: "You had to buy quite a few of them to actually select them because the actual design of the box was a very, very basic design and a wide tolerance and the actual topography of the circuit, to the circuit configuration, was such that it varied the temperature. So it was very, very hard to find one that really suited Jimi, so I came up with some modifications and analyzed the good one and then further refined the selection process of the device." Mayer adds, "Most of the recordings in the studio were done with one or two amplifiers, with a fuzzbox in front of them. I'd also given Jimi a treble booster that actually went in front of some of the fuzzboxes as well."

Chkiantz has slightly painful memories about the complications Mayer's gadgets brought to the proceedings: "I know that Hendrix had what seemed like a zillion fuzzboxes and he would chain them together. There was a lot of magic leads going on. There would be a lot of trial between the guitar, the fuzzboxes. He'd be trying to get this and also trying to get the feedback and the tone to work but to work controllably. The whole system was really quite an unstable one. Remember that he would have compressors in the guitar chain anyway, so the guitar would tend to pick up. Very easily it would take off. And then he had all the things that guitarists have: clicks on the strings when he put his fingers on them, leads that didn't work, or amplifiers that suddenly took off. He worked very hard, but he definitely had an idea about what he wanted to get and I think he communicated that successfully because Eddie obviously knew when they were going in the right direction. And they'd work on it and work on it and work on it and for us in the background, sometimes it just seemed crazy." Yet Chkiantz freely admits that while his memories of these sessions are largely ones of hanging around waiting while this gadget was adjusted or that instrument tuned, the Experience actually spent very little time in the studio compared to the other acts he would work with: "It was stunningly little when I think of how many things we tried and did." Mayer observes, "Jimi was extremely quick in the studio anyway. Overdubs and solos were taken at what today would be considered absolutely ridiculously quick [speeds]."

Though the song "Fire" featured some attention-arresting playing from Hendrix, it is a song even more noteworthy for the contribution of Mitch Mitchell. On the track partly inspired by the Redding family fireplace, the Experience's drummer was allowed to let rip, hogging center stage with some inspired and elongated skin bashing. As with many of the album's songs, the arrangement was devised on the night of recording. "We did the same thing," remembers Redding. "Hendrix and I would sit down and learn the thing." Mitchell's extended contribution seemed like a good idea: "We just thought, 'Leave those spaces open,' and Hendrix did his vocal and featured Mitchell." Some surviving outtakes of "Fire" are surprisingly conventional, with Hendrix's guitar riffs quite bright and "poppy." Only after a few takes did the more biting tone of the familiar version arise. A couple of the later "Fire" takes from the session feature extraordinarily different guitar solos than the one that was eventually used: on them, Hendrix's guitar has a much louder, bigger, and more solid quality, akin to his solos in the *Electric Ladyland* period. The solos are also lengthier.

The other track recorded this evening was an ultimately discarded "The Wind Cries Mary." Several takes were attempted. The only one that has leaked out is an altogether more smooth and confident backing track than the slightly stiff officially issued version. In addition, Hendrix's guitar is more belligerent, while Mitchell heightens the song's atmosphere with interesting work on the bass drum. Rejected because it was felt that the De Lane Lea recording had more "feel," to these ears this version—discounting its lack of vocal—is far superior to the one released.

Extraordinary (and ultimately acclaimed) as the music recorded at Hendrix's first Olympic session may be, Chkiantz did not leave the studio with especially overawed feelings. "My particular way of looking at people working in the studio is I try very hard not to judge," he reasons. "It's afterwards that I'll make up my mind whether I like it or not. Because otherwise, what are you going to do? You'd have a band come in that you don't like. You'll cripple that band if you feel that way." He does acknowledge, though, that in comparison to other acts, "Hendrix was much more interesting because we had something to do. We were playing around with backwards tapes and stuff. There were loads of ideas flying around."

Chkiantz admits that although he worked a lot with Hendrix that year, he continued to be almost as much of a stranger to him as he was on that first session: "Jimi was very shy, so one didn't get to talk to him that much 'til quite a lot later. He could cope with Eddie, he could cope with Chas, but the rest, I don't know. Maybe he didn't quite trust us, didn't quite know what to make of us."

After yet another exhilaratingly productive night in the studio, it was back to mundane reality for the Experience on February 4 as they played gigs at both the Ram Jam Club and the Flamingo Club. A tape of the Flamingo performance has turned up on bootleg. It reveals that, despite Hendrix's now prolific writing rate, the band's set was still mostly comprised of covers. "Can You See Me" and "Stone Free" are the only original numbers in a nine-song set, the rest of which is made up by "Killing Floor" (the opening number), "Have Mercy," "Like a Rolling Stone," "Rock Me Baby," "Catfish Blues," "Hey Joe," and (the set closer) "Wild Thing."

"Hey Joe" was by now up to its peak position on any chart it had hit: number six. Pleasing though this must have been to Hendrix, one wonders whether that debut now sounded positively prehistoric to him compared to the revolutionary sounds he was currently taping. After more gigs on the 5th and 6th, more recording work was done on the 7th, but there is confusion as to the studio used. Most reference books state that on this day the Experience went to Olympic to record vocal overdubs for "Purple Haze." Redding's diary entry, however, reads: "Recording, 7 'til 1 o'clock, Kingsway. Did three numbers." It's possible that the "Purple Haze" vocals were done on the 8th at Olympic (some kind of overdubs are known to have been done to the track on that day there). Whichever day they were added, it was an occasion where Chkiantz became (along with Kramer) the latest studio employee to realize that Hendrix's confidence on guitar was in inverse proportion to his happiness with his vocal abilities: "We kind of walled him off with high screens. He didn't like to be seen. It was difficult because we did quite a lot of drop-ins and we'd be trying to take a cue from Jimi and the lights would be so low we couldn't really see him. I don't know why he was so embarrassed about it. He did not really have a problem, I think." Not with his voice, perhaps, but he certainly did with the studio's wire-bridged headphones. "There's Jimi with his hair and he puts on a set of headphones that could have been easily calculated as a torture chamber for him," recalls Chkiantz. "Come to the end of a take, he'd try to take his headphones off: bloody wire would have got caught up in his hair, he'd be pulling his hair out. It was awful. You had to go down and rescue him sometimes. Just to get out of this to come back for a playback. On top of everything else they were absolutely dreadful—terrible-sounding cans."

The Olympic session on the 8th was a substantial affair. As well as recording overdubs on "Foxy Lady" and "Purple Haze," the Experience recorded "Remember," Hendrix's tribute to his chitlin circuit/R & B roots, and a song called "Midnight Lightning." The latter recording was—like "Here He Comes"/"Lover Man"—another song that Hendrix never quite seemed to be able to nail to his satisfaction in his lifetime. Not to be confused with another Experience song called "Midnight," it was frequently played live by Hendrix, but a studio version was not issued until 1975.

Though its musical style was something Hendrix knew like the back of his hand, Redding recalls that the guitarist was slightly vague about the arrangement of "Remember," the song that was almost a composite of all the lovelorn R & B numbers he'd played live in his early twenties. "Hendrix just had A to E or whatever, he had no riff," says Redding. "So I went *dang-dang-du-dang dang*, and that became the riff throughout the song." There were at least five takes of "Remember" attempted (excluding false starts), some of which broke down. One of them was taken at a markedly slower pace than the familiar one, but aside from that take there are no surprises, though one of them comes to a clean end, as opposed to a fade-out, as does an alternate mix of the master version, with an afterword in the form of one of Hendrix's "My Boy Lollipop"-style mouth pops.

Similar pops can be heard in the finished "Purple Haze." An alternate recording of that track—available on the 2000 CD box set—shows just how hard the Experience worked to perfect its songs. Featuring a different—but fine—Hendrix vocal, different guitar parts, and a less "exotic" EQing (as well as an extended fade-out where Hendrix can be heard laughing with delight and exclaiming "Freak out!"), it could just as easily have been the master take as the one we are familiar with. The overdubs were recorded again, however, until it was perfect. (A different—though less noticeably so—mix of "Foxy Lady" is also featured on the 2000 set.)

Chkiantz was by now becoming weary of the sheer volume of the Experience. "It's not very easy to listen to a few thousand watts of fuzz guitar," he says. "Sometimes, it got so loud we'd turn the [control booth] monitors off and there was really very little difference. One day as a joke I remember putting screens up in front of the control room window—on the grounds that we might like to hear something in the control room out of the speakers and not just straight through the glass." The tape op reveals that any time Hendrix came up against a problem in getting his desired sound, his first instinct would be to add another Marshall stack. "I thought that was stupid," he says simply. Chkiantz wasn't the only one with misgivings about the band's volume. Despite the fact that Olympic boasted seven or eight layers of soundproofing—essential for a studio that recorded classical strings and was located under a flight path into London Airport (as Heathrow Airport was generally known in those days)—it wasn't just the studio employees who were treated to the likes of "Purple Haze." "We had endless complaints from the neighbors," Chkiantz recollects. "We had to go 'round and close all the doors and vents and windows and God knows what. I used to walk around the outside of the studio to see how bad it was."

There were others who looked askance at the noise Hendrix made, by no means all of them from "straight" circles. Chkiantz again: "I seem to recall a lot of musicians, a lot of people, saying, 'Well, I can't see what all the fuss is about myself,' or, 'God, I don't know how you can listen to all that noise, I'd be scared to work with him.' Things like that. Chas was convinced he was on to something. Not everybody was convinced that Chas was right."

And yet, as Chkiantz noticed, despite these horrified reactions to the music Hendrix was creating, Chandler perceived Hendrix not as an avant-garde proposition but as a pop idol. This involved a honing down of Hendrix's visions: "Definitely Chas wanted records that he could sell. He needed records that he could sell. He dragooned into and eventually taught Hendrix the value of the three-minute single, three-and-a-half." Keith Altham confirms Chkinatz's memory of Chandler streamlining Hendrix's visions.

A further thing that made the Hendrix sessions rather hard work from Chkiantz's point of view were would-be gatecrashers, which Hendrix was now becoming famous enough to attract: "Hendrix did not keep it a secret where he was going. It was extraordinary. I worked with the Stones, I worked with the Beatles, I worked with Led Zeppelin. I was not as jumpy, it was not as difficult, as with Hendrix. It was something of an open house. Hendrix himself was not difficult at all, but I personally would have preferred not to have a load of girls lurking in the woodwork and so on. I had to go and get rid of them. [It was] not as much at the *Are You Experienced* sessions, but I don't recall a time after which it suddenly got worse." Hendrix was more or less oblivious to the problems his lax mouth was causing: "We kept them out of the control room and studio room where they were working."

Whatever misgivings he may have had about Hendrix's recording methods or fans, Chkiantz was beginning to realize that as a guitarist the American was something special: "He had enormous fluidity on the electric guitar. He basically could make the thing do anything. What impressed me with Davy Graham, which I didn't see with Hendrix, was he played the guitar fretboard somehow as if it was a keyboard. There was a kind of freedom. You weren't conscious of him using chord shapes at all: his fingers just seemed to run around with complete freedom on the fretboard. I don't think [Hendrix] had quite as much freedom—the electric guitar is a different instrument, of course—but it seemed to me it was more related to patterns somehow. On the other hand, he had oodles more soul, oodles more rhythm. It was clear that this guy could do just incredible things. He was a virtuoso. Prior to that, the electric guitar was not the world's most enthralling instrument, frankly. To me, it often seemed a limited device."

As for Hendrix's rhythm section, Chkiantz—like Mike Ross-Trevor at CBS—got the impression quite quickly that their status was adjacent to those of hired hands: "In the very early days, they were definitely the sub act and that was the deal. I think Noel felt himself to be crippled by the thing for some time. Drummers on music sessions always get heaved out of the picture as soon as they've done the drums. They've got a way of living with that. Bass players have exactly the same problem, but because they're playing a tuned instrument they tend to get involved in production and worrying. Well, Noel didn't have a chance to do that." This notwithstanding, he noticed the pair were, in their limited roles, given a freedom that implied a trust in their abilities: "I wouldn't have sworn that I've ever seen Hendrix say, 'These are the chords.' He just played and expected them to find their way."

A gig at the Bromel Club took place on this day. There were then gigs at four different venues on February 9–12 inclusive, all outside London. On February 13, the Experience played another BBC radio session, performing the A- and B-sides of their debut single plus a couple of previews of tracks from the album in progress, "Love or Confusion" and "Foxy Lady." The performances were for *Saturday Club* and would be broadcast five days later. Exposure on *Saturday Club* was arguably even more important than television appearances: the program was heard by approximately nine million people each week, an astonishing figure for a country with a population below 60 million. All these tracks can be heard on the CD *BBC Sessions*.

There were Experience gigs on February 14, 15, 17, and 18. The latter performance was at the Art College, University of York, and was an utterly miserable affair for the band. They set off at 5:00 PM in Mitchell's car but did not arrive at the venue until midnight, due to the car breaking down. Meanwhile, the beginnings of real disquiet in the Hendrix camp about remuneration were illustrated by the circumstances surrounding their pay raise to £30 per week, which they received upon their return to London (where they played the Blarney Club on the 19th). A second pay raise in the space of a month may sound generous, but it had been prompted by the Experience threatening to go on strike if their financial situation did not show immediate improvement. "I wrote a letter on behalf of the band," says Redding. "I found out how much money we were earning." Redding had the most cause to be particularly sore over the disparity between the gig fees he was meticulously noting in his diary and his personal income: he was having to pay rent, while Mitchell was still living with his parents.

Though Olympic was by consensus the best studio the Experience had yet visited, Hendrix was not prepared to wait on his muse if the studio was, for whatever reason, unavailable. "When Jimi wanted to go into the studio late at night, you had to find an amenable engineer that would [say] 'Yes, I'll stay late at night,'" says Etchingham. "And often Eddie Kramer didn't want to stay late at night, 'cos I used to make the phone calls to book the studios. He used to book them at short notice." Chkiantz suggests another reason for the Experience not using Olympic exclusively: "Time at Olympic was like gold dust. You had one studio that was working twenty hours a day. It was booked out about two months ahead." Consequently, on February 20, after playing a gig in Bath, the

Experience returned to De Lane Lea to record "I Don't Live Today." "It's in C sharp and it was quite a hard track to do," is Redding's laconic recollection of one of *Are You Experienced*'s most way out and effects-drenched songs. There were at least four takes of the basic track recorded. All of them are extraordinary for the way they show that the weird and wonderful sounds and effects to be heard on the master version are not particularly dependent on overdubs at all: Hendrix changes guitar tone in the blink of an eye, and moves in and out of feedback with equal ease. On this track, Hendrix used a hand wah-wah, a precursor of the pedal-operated device, which lends a wailing tone to a guitar's sound. One take, possibly the earliest, is particularly interesting because Hendrix's riff is not the staccato and sharp sound of the album version but something more sinuous and distorted, which then melds almost seamlessly into his rhythm work. Unfortunately, this track breaks down at about the two-and-a-half minute mark. The band proceeded to try something less pleasing on the ear in the subsequent takes, including the one used for the master.

On February 22, the Experience played "Hey Joe" on the BBC radio show *Parade of the Pops*. They then played at both the Speakeasy and the Roundhouse in London. As if to add insult to the injury of the farcical University of York gig, Hendrix's guitar was stolen at the Roundhouse. Chandler had to sell another bass to get him a replacement. The following day, the band performed in Worthing before traveling to De Lane Lea and laying down "Manic Depression." For many, Redding's upward-spiraling basslines on this incendiary track are at least as compelling as Hendrix's guitar or Mitchell's *1812 Overture* drumming. "Not many people can play that,"

Redding says proudly of his contribution. There were at least three takes, although one of them broke down very quickly. The two that weren't used for the master are significantly different than the familiar version. Whereas on the *Are You Experienced* master there is a silent pause before the repetition of the three-note intro, on the outtakes Mitchell fills the pause with a drum roll. On the alternate version that doesn't break down, the ending is a complete contrast to the measured stages of the master's close. Instead, this take features an elongated sonic chaos of guitar squall, feedback wail, and drum-kit pulverization before ebbing slowly into silence with cymbal tinkles.

Gigs followed on the 24th, 25th, and 26th (the latter seeing the Experience acting as one of the support acts to lightweight pop act Dave Dee, Dozy, Beaky, Mick, & Titch). Some sources claim that on the 26th the Experience went into Olympic and recorded a 12-bar, horn-augmented jam and a song called "Gypsy Blood." This is almost certainly erroneous (Redding: "I'd remember if we had a horn section"), and would seem to have resulted from mislabeled tape boxes. (It's possible that they were in fact recorded on February 26, 1969: the Experience worked in Olympic that day and one of the tracks recorded was "Gypsy Blood," as well as what are described as "Jams and Outtakes.") On the 27th, Redding went into De Lane Lea for more recording, only to discover that he was the sole person to turn up for the session. The session was canceled.

the release

MARCH 1, 1967, SAW THE EXPERIENCE engaging in one of its rare rehearsals, this one at the Speakeasy. Between 2:00 P.M. and 5:00 P.M., they attended De Lane Lea where they attempted a recording of "Like a Rolling Stone." According to Chandler, the Experience never managed to lay down a releasable version of Bob Dylan's classic because Mitchell was never able to stay in time on it: he would either be speeding up or slowing down, to the frustration of his colleagues. The tape has never surfaced. The attempt was probably pointless in any event. The melancholic live Monterey festival version that was first released on the 1970 Otis Redding/Jimi Hendrix album *Historic Performances* only serves to confirm that even an artist of the stature of Hendrix could not hope to match (let alone surpass) the hair-raising power of the venomous original. Hendrix would have been better advised to try to record a studio version of his rapid-fire take on "Killing Floor."

This unproductive session was the Experience's last visit to any recording studio for almost a month. Instead, they devoted their time to live performances and promotional work.

On March 3, the Experience flew to Paris for a short tour of Europe involving both gigs and media interviews. On their return on the 8th, they launched into a series of domestic gigs, including two shows at the Club A Go Go, the Newcastle club owned by Jeffery. It was back over to Europe on the 13th for an appearance on the Dutch TV show *Fanclub* on the 14th. The Experience was back in London in time to attend Track Records' launch party at the Speakeasy on the

16th. The following day saw said label's first official release: "Purple Haze," backed with "51st Anniversary," by the Jimi Hendrix Experience. Not that the band had time to savor this, because they were now traveling again, this time for a short residency at the Star Club in Hamburg. At the end of the three-night Star Club residency, the band flew to Luxembourg to do a Radio Luxembourg interview, and flew back to London the next day.

The new single was even more impressive than the Experience's not-at-all disgraceful debut. This extended to the flip side of the record: although it explores the same theme as the previous single's B-side, "51st Anniversary" is, unlike "Stone Free," much more antimarriage than antiwoman or antirelationship. It is also on entirely another level musically: a gritty, uptempo track with some tension-building blurred-handed guitar from Hendrix. The composer—after a first verse in which long term and happy marriages are acknowledged—evokes the misery of two mutually hostile people trapped in a union for perpetuity via images of children who receive no attention or affection from either a mother who is too wrapped up in misery or a father who is too busy blotting out his unhappiness at the whiskey house.

"Purple Haze," meanwhile, was a concoction of dazzling verbal imagery and breathtakingly raucous music that sounded like nothing ever heard before in rock 'n' roll history. Aesthetically brilliant, it also demanded attention through its very differentness. The record wasn't completely alien to prevailing pop trends, however. That very month saw the formation proper of Procol Harum, whose "A Whiter Shade of Pale" would be one of the anthems of the imminent Summer of Love. Similarly, the March chart debut of the far from ordinary John's Children, and the announcement that same month that Stevie Winwood was leaving the Spencer Davis Group to set up the band that would become Traffic, indicated that pop winds were carrying a rather exotic fragrance. Yet even in this shimmering climate, "Purple Haze" managed to sound other-dimensional.

"When I heard 'Purple Haze' I said, 'My God, man—what is this?'" recalls Vic Briggs. "I was definitely blown away by 'Purple Haze.' There wasn't a lot of hard rock things going on on the Brit charts. Even rock hits like 'I Want to Hold Your Hand' or 'She Loves You,' it didn't have this gutsy, bluesy, driving sound that 'Purple Haze' did." Roger Mayer points out: "The reaction from that single took Jimi completely into another level. That really got some attention." For Chkiantz, the release of "Purple Haze" put his mind to rest as to whether all the hard work on the intricacies of the music were worthwhile: "I was really quite surprised at how much of it actually came out on the radio, because when you heard what was coming out of the studio speakers you thought, 'This is never coming out . . . not a chance.'"

Stamp is convinced that the artistic blossoming of Hendrix that "Purple Haze" so dramatically demonstrated simply could not have happened in the guitarist's native land. "When we saw Jimi, Jimi, apart from his hair, rather looked like an R & B star," he points out. "He wore suits and things. I said to Chas, 'Let's get Jimi on the King's Road. Let him see Ozzie Clarke. Let him go to all the great stores that are just beginning and all the new young designers.' What happened to Jimi in London and what enabled him to sing, what enabled him to write and all those things, was . . . he suddenly found himself in a supportive community of Track, of Chas, of having a group of his own and then meeting designers and things who suggested things to him. He was also an enormously exotic being. So immediately he started to realize that he could go anywhere here. I never saw anyone put a bandana on his head before Jimi. He put them on his arms so that they were moving as he did his arm movements. He came into his own essence in London, because in America he was like some sort of nigger—even though he was a musician. He had that guarded, defensive thing. He was restricted by his own birthplace. Suddenly he had the safety and also the caring and the nurturing of creative people around him who said: 'Go, man! Write songs. Sing. Look incredible. Do this. Do more, do more, do more.'"

On March 21, the same day that the Experience played the Speakeasy again, Mike Jeffery signed a contract for the Experience's records to be released in the United States by Warner subsidiary Reprise Records. Reprise was a strange choice. The label had originally been set up by Frank Sinatra, but had been bought by Warner when it experienced financial difficulties in 1963. Prior to the Experience's first album, it had no experience of releasing rock records. Reprise was signing not just an act who was unknown Stateside, but who were essentially unknown to *them*: the label's Stan Cornyn has subsequently admitted that Reprise was simply trying to break into the rock field. Jeffery took advantage of their naivety to get the Experience—or, rather, himself—a reported advance of $120,000, a staggering amount for a new group, even despite their chart successes in Britain.

While Jeffery was making his deals, Hendrix, Etchingham, Chandler, and Lotta were involved in the more mundane matter of moving house. The boisterousness of their household had ensured enough complaints to make them *personas non grata* at Montagu Square. The four decamped to a flat in Upper Berkeley Street, located in Mayfair, London. As at their previous flat, the two couples had their respective privacy: the new flat was big and had two bathrooms.

There was a gig on March 22 in Southampton. The following day, "Purple Haze" entered the U.K. charts, a far quicker showing than the slow-burning "Hey Joe" had managed. After gigs outside London on the 25th and 26th, the Experience promoted the new single on the 27th by recording a performance for TV show *Dee Time* in Manchester. The single was guaranteed more exposure following another recording of it for *Saturday Club* on March 28 ("Fire" and "Killing Floor" were the other tracks recorded for the program) before the Experience journeyed to Aylesbury for a gig. The Experience finally resumed work on *Are You Experienced* on March 29. At De Lane Lea, they recorded the American version of "Red House," "La Poupee Quit Fait Non," and a mystery track called "Teddy Bears Live Forever." They also did some more work, probably overdubs and/or mixing, on "Manic Depression."

Why Hendrix or Chandler wanted to take another stab at "Red House" is a mystery. The version recorded on December 13 is so good it seems unimprovable. The presence of light echo effects and some guitar overdubs on the master that emerged from the March session suggests that one or both of them thought the first version too "bare." At least four takes were attempted. The studio chatter on surviving outtakes indicates a good-humored session. The outtakes also reveal that Hendrix would seem to have by now found a way to prevent the instruments from bleeding into his vocal track: he sang live on the takes. Those who marvel at the ability of musicians to sing and play at the same time will be reduced to slack-jawed amazement at the way Hendrix demonstrates on these takes that he can lay down his vocal while simultaneously producing some of the most awe-inspiring guitar work ever heard. Also stunning is the way that Hendrix's guitar lines change from take to take: he is truly improvising as he goes along.

Take one (assuming that the takes that have leaked out are the only ones attempted) is rather hesitant, especially vocally, and appropriately enough breaks down just as Hendrix has sung the "wait a minute, something's wrong . . ." line. Chandler is heard advising, "Keep the rhythm just going on the chords . . ." The next take is another rather fumbling performance—despite the exquisite fretboard explorations—and breaks down not long after the previous take did. Somebody whistles to signify dissatisfaction, and Chandler says, "Start again." "Yeah," Hendrix agrees and laments, "Once I hit that wrong note . . ." Take three is a smoother performance, but the guitar solo is rather feeble compared to the way it soars on the U.S. and (especially) U.K. masters. Significantly, it is straight after that solo that the performance peters out. There is another exchange between the control room and the studio, with Hendrix, half laughing, saying, "One little thing throws me off." Not entirely seriously, Hendrix then suggests it is the studio lights distracting him, presumably a reference to his preference for singing in the dark. Chandler says he isn't allowed to turn any more lights off because of the fire exit. "In other words, we're making up all the smoke in here?" says Hendrix in mirth. "We're cooking—is that what you're trying to say?" They were certainly cooking on the next try: this take was used for the master of the U.S. version.

This track has been removed from the 1997 "international edition" *Are You Experienced* CD in favor of the U.K. version, but the American version of the song still remains on the U.S. version of that CD (as does the original American running order, albeit with the other missing tracks from the U.K. edition added as bonus tracks). Those non-U.S. residents who want to hear this nifty alternate version of the song (not quite as good as the U.K. version—but, then, not much is) should consult the 1997 CD *Experience Hendrix: The Best of Jimi Hendrix*. Americans who wish to hear the British version should seek out either the international edition of *Are You Experienced* or the *Jimi Hendrix: Blues* album.

"La Poupée Qui Fait Non"—also known as "No No No" but with an approximate English translation of "The Doll Who Says No"—is a composition by French pop idol Michel Polnareff in collaboration with one F. Gerald. The Experience had heard Polnareff perform it on the Dutch *Fanclub* show and had started playing it themselves. The single take that has leaked out is a vocal-less, jangly, folk-rockish affair. It's difficult to imagine it was seriously intended for the album. Possibly it was just done to get everyone in the mood for recording. As for "Teddy Bears Live Forever," Noel

Redding—who is said to play guitar on it—can remember nothing about it. No take has leaked out, but it seems safe to assume that it was an ice-breaking jam that just happened to be given a name on the tape box.

After a performance of "Purple Haze" on *Top of the Pops* on March 30 (which consisted of live vocals over a studio backing track), the Experience joined a bizarre package tour. Starting on the last day of that month, the tour saw the band supporting the Walker Brothers, Cat Stevens, and Redding's old acquaintance, Engelbert Humperdinck. Even for a package tour—a multi-artist bill concept just about to expire in a psychedelic flame as rock audiences became savvy to being treated with contempt by promoters—it was a spectacular mismatch of styles and temperaments. This was illustrated by the events that occurred at the first performance, at the Astoria in London. Hendrix—at the suggestion of Keith Altham—decided that the best way to grab some attention and publicity was by setting his guitar on fire. The other acts treated the Experience with suspicion throughout the rest of the tour.

On April 1, the tour played the Odeon in Ipswich. On this night, Redding started moonlighting as guitarist for Humperdinck, whose own guitarist had walked off the tour. Redding would play hidden in the wings. After the tour's stop at the Gaumont in Worcester the following day, there was a gap in the itinerary, of which the Experience took advantage to make the final recordings for *Are You Experienced* at Olympic.

The session on the 3rd was something of a marathon, lasting from 6:30 P.M. until 3:00 A.M. the following morning. In these eight and a half hours, the Experience laid down "Are

You Experienced," "May This Be Love," "Highway Chile," an unfinished basic track given the name "Title #3," a demo of a song called "Go My Own Way" (which is unreleased to date), and a stab at Leiber & Stoller's "Hound Dog" (also unreleased). In addition, overdubs and mixing work were done on "Love or Confusion" and a lead vocal overdubbed onto "Fire."

Although what would become the title track of the album was one of the last songs to be recorded, evidence shows that the title (and possibly the whole song) had been in Hendrix's head for quite a while. In March 1967, the new Animals had recorded a song called "Yes, I Am Experienced" for their debut album *Winds of Change*, which was released in September 1967. Vic Briggs recalls that the Animals' song was given this title, and its lyric was written by Eric Burdon, before February 1967. Remarkably, Burdon had written another lyric that referred to Hendrix even before that. In January 1967 the new Animals recorded the title track of their first LP, a roll call of modern recording artists in which Burdon enunciates: "Now that we got Jimi Hendrix, we know where we are." So Burdon had written two celebrations of Hendrix's talent when the only Hendrix product in the stores was "Hey Joe." "When we started rehearsing *Yes, I Am Experienced*, it took me a while before I connected that it was about Jimi Hendrix, because I was thinking music," says Briggs. "'What? This guy's written a tribute song to somebody who hasn't even come out with an album? What the fucking hell?'" On a pedantic note, the title track of the U.S. edition of *Are You Experienced* was given a question mark (as indeed, on the spine at least, was the album title) by the U.S. record label.

Said title track was a psychedelic extravaganza. Hendrix himself disliked his music being referred to by that term, but by just about every criteria, the track fit the profile of the records released in the last year or so that were bracketed in that genre. Psychedelia was a genre of music that could not have happened without two things: the growing popularity of LSD; and the increasing sophistication of studio technology. These two elements were inextricably intertwined: weird and wonderful sounds that could now be generated from instruments and mixing consoles were employed to give an approximation of the surreal experiences obtained by ingesting lysergic acid diethylamide, the latest drug of choice for the pop aristocracy. Not that all psychedelia was inspired by acid trips: many consider the Yardbirds' ominous, exotic early-1966 single "Shapes of Things" to be the first example of psychedelia, and that was probably inspired by nothing more than a few pints of English bitter and a weariness of 12-bar blues progressions. By 1967, psychedelia was in full swing on both sides of the Atlantic. This was inevitably assisted by the the Beatles—the standard bearers for all popular music—who experimented with backward tapes on "Rain," and flirted with hippies via allusions to the acid-head bible *The Tibetan Book of the Dead* in the lyric to "Tomorrow Never Knows." Rather than innovating as such, however, the Fab Four were following the lead of the Byrds, particularly their eerie, gliding 1966 single "Eight Miles High." Where the Byrds and the Beatles trod, hundreds followed, and anyone and everyone were soon trying to out-weird each other, often in a monkey see, monkey do manner. This was perhaps best exemplified in Britain by records such as "Stop, Stop,

Stop," in which the clean-cut Hollies shoehorned effects and a vaguely Eastern time signature into their usual giddy pop format. Psychedelic music in America (where the term psychedelia was at the time simply used to refer to hippie paraphernalia and culture) was less contrived, but somehow also less fun: in San Francisco, a flower power scene that was just about to break nationally boasted acts including the Grateful Dead, Jefferson Airplane, and the Quicksilver Messenger Service, who engaged in free-form jamming and blatant drug references. The parameters of the music were even wide enough to encompass Steppenwolf's "Magic Carpet Ride" on the grounds that it was a longish jam-sounding record with unusual noises. The song "Are You Experienced" featured a lyric that alluded to drug taking and free sex, as well as a backward guitar, strange effects, and an EQing deliberately designed to produce a thoroughly surre-al air. The same was true of "Love or Confusion," "I Don't Live Today" and "3rd Stone from the Sun," but of the four songs, the title track was the most way out.

Although Hendrix may have had the basic idea for the title track far back enough for Burdon to have already writ-ten an answer song, according to Roger Mayer, who was present at the session, the overdub-heavy final production was so dependent on moments of inspiration and improvisa-tion that parts of the song were effectively written in the studio. "Because as the effects happened, or the sound happened, that would definitely give rise to what you could actually do in the mix," he says. "They are quite closely inter-twined: how do you know you're gonna do a sound 'til you've created a sound? You don't, so the first thing you do is create the sound and then figure out what to do with it."

The track's backward guitar solo created more headaches for Kramer and Chkiantz. "The real difficulty is figuring out what to provide as a guide track," explains Chkiantz. "How to know where you are in the song, because you turn the tape over so the track's now playing backwards. Now the question is, where's the downbeat? We perceive the downbeat as when it goes *boop*, not when it goes *shuuuck*. Where do you start on that?" Yet this was far less of a problem to Hendrix, who seemed to know in his head what his backward guitar would sound like. Chkiantz: "He wasn't sort of surprised at the results. It always appeared to be more or less what he expected. Or he might say, 'Oh, that's wrong' and then he'd go back and figure out what to do about it in order to make it work. Some people have a knack. I don't think he was thrashing around for anything that worked. I think he did have a concept of the sounds that he wanted."

"Title #3" finally saw the light of day 33 years later on the 2000 CD box set. It turned out to be a pleasant enough but unremarkable uptempo track with an intro similar to Hendrix's version of "Killing Floor" and a riff reminiscent of the guitar work in "Can You See Me." "Love or Confusion" was subjected to some overdubs that made it sound very different from the unadorned basic track. As Redding remembers, "I used a backwards bass, he used a backwards guitar, because we were all influenced by the Beatles."

It was a thoroughly productive session, but Chkiantz got the impression that such lightning recording processes were the result of an unhealthy pressure applied by Chandler. "I saw him as a restriction on Hendrix," he says. "Now I appreciate that somebody or other had to tie his feet to somewhere near Earth, and that certainly when Hendrix wandered off he didn't achieve as much in many ways as he did with Chas, but my feeling was that he was hustled a bit into getting things done and that you could still have got things done without being quite so heavy-handed about it. [Chas] was okay as long as he thought he was getting somewhere and, actually, to give him his due, he was quite patient if he could see that it was difficult for Jimi to play. Chas didn't want the bills to run away. He pushed to keep things moving. I think Jimi would probably have had to fight for another take a bit. If Jimi said, 'No, that's not it at all,' then, mistake or no mistake, it wouldn't be used, but if Jimi was uncertain—which is, after all, very often what happens—then Chas would say, 'Look, it's good enough, we can overdub this.'" This hustling by Chandler has, for Chkiantz, led to a lasting scar across Hendrix's musical legacy: "I thought that there was a tendency for them to go with the first thing that would pass. Me personally, I'm not too happy with the quality on Hendrix's recordings. There are too many studio jokes, too many, 'Oh well, we don't want it to sound too clinical, so we'll leave this mistake in or that fluff in.' He plays wrong notes. I think it's very sad that what we're now left with are flawed diamonds."

When the band returned to Olympic the next day, they took another stab at getting a satisfactory take of "Here He Comes"/"Lover Man" and did overdubs and mixing work on "3rd Stone from the Sun" and "Highway Chile." A vocal-less take of "Here He Comes"/"Lover Man" recorded this day was another track that would first see the light of day on the 2000 CD box set. In truth, it's a below average number, whether it be in the bare-bones rendition heard on the 2000 set or the post-*Electric Ladyland* version that is available on *South Saturn Delta*. The latter, fully realized with vocals, reveals that it has only the sketchiest of melodies and a general feeling of going nowhere about it. Had it been included on *Are You Experienced*, it would have weakened the album.

In contrast to the lack of progress on "Here He Comes"/ "Lover Man," "Highway Chile" was given overdubs and a mix that created a finished track only a day after it had been started. "3rd Stone from the Sun" also had overdubs and mixing work done to it, but this was not as straightforward a process. So extensive was the overdubbing work done on this day that it virtually became a new recording. Both Chandler and Kramer later recalled that almost nothing was kept from the January 11 take of "3rd Stone . . ." As Roger Mayer, who was in attendance, points out, "That was painting a picture of the movement and the spaceship sounds." In order to help paint the picture, Hendrix added more backward guitar parts. Mayer: "The backing track was put on forwards, then the tape was turned over—because your tape recorders don't run backwards, so what you actually do is you flip the tape over—and then Jimi put on the other guitar part. And then the tape's flipped back the other way so the backing track's 'round the right way." Chkiantz and Mayer agree that the backward insertions and consequent effects were anything but arbitrary. Hendrix placed the guitar part precisely where he wanted it to go, and was always aware of just how the part would affect the sonic landscape. "We were always quite amazed that Jimi knew where he was with the song," says Mayer.

The phrase "mixing" acquired more than one meaning when the vocals were added to "3rd Stone . . ." A dialogue between Hendrix and Chandler, in which Hendrix played a starfleet officer and Chandler a crewman on a scoutship, was recorded, slowed down to incomprehensibility, and added to the stew of swirling guitar, feedback, and special effects. Said dialogue, therefore, became like an ingredient in a soup, losing its own distinct properties but bringing something to the overall flavor. Those listeners who played their vinyl record at 78 rpm could hear the words in real time. The dialogue is also featured at real-time speed on the 2000 CD box set, along with a first take of it where Chandler (probably the only alien who has ever had a Newcastle accent) caused Hendrix to crack up with laughter by fluffing his lines. Kramer assisted the song's surreal air by bringing Mitchell's cymbals forward in the mix. Part of the song's extraordinary rhythm track consisted of a tolling sound that is actually Hendrix playing octaves on an upright piano.

The end result of all this experimentation is, to Hendrix's gizmo man, the album's most unique offering. "That was the most psychedelic track," Mayer opines. "That kind of set the tone for the next album, *Axis*. It actually pointed the overall direction and the type of sounds because that was the beginning of the Summer of '67 love thing, that's when it was all kicking off. It was a groundbreaking track."

From the sublime to the ridiculous: after completing the tracks for probably the most innovative album yet recorded, the Experience returned the next day to the Walker Brothers tour. Redding has observed that playing guitar for Humperdinck and then bass for Hendrix each evening was like being bounced back and forth in a time warp, such was the contrast between the two styles of music. There were gigs in Leeds, Glasgow, Carlisle, Derbyshire, and Liverpool before Hendrix and Chandler returned to Olympic on the 9th (the same day as the Liverpool gig) for final mixing. The mixing continued on the 10th, a day on which the Experience also performed "Purple Haze" and "Foxy Lady" for a live broadcast of *BBC Playhouse Theatre*. Redding and Mitchell would seem to have been offered no part in the mixing, although Redding points out, "I wasn't interested in it." The mixing process involved the remixing of songs recorded at the several other studios the Experience had used during the album's gestation, something vital to avoid jarringly different sound levels and qualities. Chkiantz: "The consistency that you see was the fact that it was all mixed in the same place."

As was only now just becoming the norm, there were two mixes prepared: mono and stereo. The stereo version would not be released in Britain until the early 1970s, although both mixes would be offered to consumers in America. This was logical. In the United States, most music consumers had a stereo record player, and stereo radio had been introduced. In the United Kingdom, very few people had stereo record players, and stereo radio was simply unheard of. There are small but noticeable differences between the stereo and mono mixes. For instance, the mono version of "May This Be Love" begins with a drum roll that is not heard on the stereo mix, while on the stereo mix there is the sound of Hendrix turning a page of lyrics at 0:57 that is inaudible on the mono version. (In addition, the original mono mix of "3rd Stone from the Sun" featured a line in the first minute—"War must be war"—

that has been edited out of all subsequent versions.)

The argument has been made by many that mono mixes from this period in history are much more powerful than stereo mixes. As Mike Ross's previous comments indicate, stereo mixes were something of an afterthought at the time. Certainly, Chris Stamp considers the mono version of *Are You Experienced* to be the real McCoy. "Knowing the way he works, that was what he was defining it as in his mind," he says. "He then started to embrace stereo but at that time the mono was the definitive version for Jimi." Even so, thanks to Kramer, the stereo mix of the album was unusually good for the period. "The mono was the more important mix, but Eddie did take his stereo slightly more seriously," reveals Chkiantz. "It was a bit later on that year [1967] that stereo became the [standard] mix." Even so, the mono version of "Manic Depression" is far more impressive than its stereo counterpart, with Mitchell's drums sounding significantly bolder and louder.

On this occasion, Chkiantz had no problem with the unusually short deadline given to the task at hand: "Left to himself, Jimi would have mixed the bloody thing for at least nine months, and it would have come out with nothing that was very different. I don't think he had enough time, but I don't think he should have had unlimited time."

It was done.

In little more than a dozen sessions—virtually each of which consisted of a snatched few hours—the Experience had recorded an LP the likes of which had never been heard. "I think Chas came up with Jimi in [our office on] Old Compton Street and we played it up there," says Chris

Stamp. "I'd heard a lot of it before that, but it was amazing. We were knocked out." With the content of the album taken care of, only the packaging was left to be arranged. The sleeve of the album's U.K. edition would feature Hendrix towering over Redding and Mitchell, his cape-draped arms spread wide in a Dracula-esque pose. "I organized the cover artwork," says Stamp. "Jim had gotten that cloak some-where—I think [from the store] Granny Takes a Trip—and I suggested a few things to take. I organized them with a pho-tographer who I trusted. And I had some guy—I think it was Alan Aldridge—who did the letters."

The photographer chosen was Bruce Fleming, a prolific pop lensman who had snapped the Hollies, the Dave Clark Five, Lulu, the Animals, and many other major acts. "That's how I met Chas," Fleming explains of his work for the latter ensemble. "He rang me up and said he liked my stuff and said, 'I want you to meet one of my new boys, come over to the office.'" Fleming subsequently attended a couple of the *Are You Experienced* recording sessions and went to some Experience gigs. Some reports have suggested that there were two shoots for the album cover, the second being neces-sitated by the results of the first being rejected by the Hendrix management because they were in black and white. Fleming is adamant that there was only one shoot specifically for the cover and says he shot in both color and mono-chrome on this day, which was sometime in February 1967, possibly the 27th. Fleming made no requests or suggestions about what the Experience should wear: "They just brought what they fancied." Chandler—who, notwithstanding Stamp's involvement in the cover design, was the point of contact for Fleming with the Hendrix camp—made only two stipulations. First, the picture had to be color. Second, "We had to show the boys, because this was their first album," Fleming explains. "It got much more esoteric as time went on, but to establish the artist we had to get their faces across so the kids recognized them."

Fleming had formulated a pose in his head that he felt would capture the essence of Hendrix's music. "His music was pretty wild, and the prevalent thing at the time was psychedelic and all things strange so you had to do something odd," the photographer reasons. "The more outrageous and outlandish you got, the better. So I went for a dark green background—deep, deep green—and then just him with his cloak up. There was an alchemy about it. There was something strange going on here, different. This was a man who was flying at night. This guy could fly, literally. That's what I tried to get across. Not Dracula, but as he wore cloaks quite a lot I thought it might be nice to incorporate the cloak." Although Hendrix looks like he is standing on a box on the finished sleeve, Fleming says his feet were planted on the floor. "He was over six foot, very long and lean," he recalls. Redding and Mitchell were kneeling: "They may have been on boxes, because kneeling they would have been too low."

Once the pictures were developed, Fleming had to make slight allowances for the room needed to add wording: "It wasn't decided where the lettering was going, but I was working on a Hasselblad, which is 6 by 6 centimeters format. So I planed it the way I felt and there was space at the top and space 'round." Fleming handed over all the shots taken at the session to Chandler, indicating the one he thought was the best. "I marked it, put a cross, and said, 'Please use that one,'" he recalls. "They said, 'Looks great.' Then I didn't hear a word—not a bloody word—and then when I saw the album I realized they'd used the wrong one. I shot a series from below looking up and they chose one where he was more or less head on and I didn't like it." Fleming describes his rejected favorite as ". . . more sinister, more interesting." The final selection would seem to have been Track's: "I was talking to Chas. He said, 'I didn't have anything to do with that.'"

Daringly, the name of the artist was not put on the album's front cover. Instead, two half moons spelled out the album title on either side of Hendrix's head, the typeface of which was a sort of halfway house between the conventional and the psychedelic. (In Continental Europe, Polydor added "Jimi Hendrix" across the top of the sleeve in the same typeface.)

With a predominant dullness of color—brown and green—and a tinge of the comical about the subject's pose, the contrast between the vitality of the album and its cover's staidness is striking. Stamp concedes this quite readily: "It's not a great cover at all. Hopefully, we made up for that in all the other covers. It was like a quick cover."

There was no question of having any of the three singles ("The Wind Cries Mary" had already been earmarked for single release) on the album. "We've already made *A Quick One* with the Who and *The Who Sell Out*," recalls Stamp. "So we're already working on the idea of "album" albums, containing the idea of what singles are. We hated that there were things called Album Tracks and they were just a word for Not That Good. We were vehemently against anything that could be considered an album of that type where you had on it any-thing that were like fillers."

The Experience spent the rest of April on the Walker Brothers tour, taking their multicolored, feedback-drenched show to the still very conservative "regions" of Britain, where even having shoulder-length hair could have one "queer-bashed." Hotel after hotel denied they had reservations in their name when they caught sight of them. The way all the other acts on the tour treated the Experience was not too dis-similar to their ordeals at the hands of pompous desk porters. The Experience retaliated by playing practical jokes on them such as firing water pistols at performing acts or releasing mechanical miniature robots onto the stage.

On the first day of May, the first Experience single was released in America: "Hey Joe," backed by "51st Anniversary." On the 4th, the same day as they mimed "Purple Haze" (with a live vocal) for *Top of the Pops*, the Experience went into Olympic and recorded an early version of "Look Over Yonder" called "Mr. Bad Luck," "Taking Care of No Business," "She's So Fine," "Cat Talking to Me," and "If Six Was Nine." *Are You Experienced* had not yet been released, but the album that would become *Axis: Bold As Love* was already being set in motion. The mind boggles at Hendrix's ceaseless creativity: there was apparently not even a thought of resting, only of putting down his Niagara Falls tumble of ideas onto tape.

The following day, "The Wind Cries Mary" became the Experience's third U.K. single. That the follow-up to "Purple Haze" should come out while "Purple Haze" was still riding high in the hit parade (and would actually reach number three in one chart, an astonishing achievement for such a raucous record) was an almost unprecedented piece of marketing. Track decided, however, that it would be a nifty strategy to demonstrate to the public the breadth of ability and vision of their artist. "We did that on purpose," says Stamp. "We actually released '. . . Wind Cries Mary' whilst 'Purple Haze' was at number three or something. We wanted musically to show who this person was. '. . . Wind Cries Mary' came out because it was so different." Such a strategy would be unthinkable today. "It was about the moment," remembers Stamp of the music scene of the time. "A single was like a daily newspaper. The message was immediate. It wasn't like this gigantic slow moving train of banks and finance that it is now."

It seems psychologically revealing that "Highway Chile," the flip side of "The Wind Cries Mary," was the third Hendrix B-side in a row to celebrate personal freedom and a lack of ties: Hendrix certainly seemed to have a terror of routine and domesticity—even though his relationship with Kathy Etchingham (though nonmonogamous) was long-term and was ultimately ended by her. "Highway Chile" was the Experience's best flip so far. The image Hendrix's lyrics paint of the loner with a guitar across his back, traversing the highways and byways, serves to turn his antipathy toward obligations and conventions from a petty jibe at clingy women into an altogether more mythical and epic kind of hankering. The mid-tempo musical backing is excellent: a guitar riff in particular is suitably dramatic for a song that has the smack of a philosophical statement. Said riff, in contrast to so many of Hendrix's, is plucked, not strummed.

"The Wind Cries Mary" was another Top Ten hit, achieving a highest position of six. It also alerted the public to the fact that the so-called Wild Man of Borneo was capable of songs of delicacy and sensitivity. Certainly, Mike Ross-Trevor was impressed: "I was very surprised. I remember thinking, 'He's turned into a pop singer now.'" Vic Briggs says, "It was almost shocking to me. It was a total departure from what he'd already done."

On Friday, May 12, 1967, *Are You Experienced* was released in Britain on Track Records, catalog number 612 001. Its release had been brought forward from the intended May 26 date after a distribution error resulted in 2,000 copies being shipped to London stores a fortnight early. Although the presence of the soundtrack of *The Sound of Music*, which was at the top of the U.K. charts at the time, might indicate otherwise, the album was released into a heady atmosphere. Three of the Rolling Stones—the second most important rock act in the world—were facing drug charges. Mick Jagger and Keith Richards had been arrested at Richards's Redlands house in a bust that would notoriously see them both imprisoned, then subsequently released following a public outcry over their discriminatorily harsh sentences. Brian Jones had also been charged with possession in a separate incident. Meanwhile, the Beatles' forthcoming new album, due to be released the following month, already had an air of mystique. That album, which everybody (correctly) expected to be cut from the same intoxicatingly baroque cloth as the recent "Strawberry Fields Forever" and "Penny Lane," was so eagerly awaited—it had been a then-unprecedented five months in the making—that 100 American radio stations were already playing four illegally leaked tracks.

Are You Experienced made its first appearance on the album charts on May 27 (while the Experience was in Braunschweig,

West Germany, coming to the end of yet another of their Continental jaunts). The album never made number one, but was probably only kept off the top spot by that much-anticipated new Beatles album, *Sgt. Pepper's Lonely Hearts Club Band*, the other psychedelic masterpiece of the summer of 1967, released three weeks after the Experience's effort. *Sgt. Pepper* held the top spot for 23 consecutive weeks. Nevertheless, *Are You Experienced* remained on the U.K. album charts for an impressive 33 weeks, and was still there when its follow-up, *Axis: Bold As Love*, made its first chart appearance.

In the second week of June, the Experience took part in a photo session at Kew Gardens, with lensman Karl Ferris. A picture from this color session would be used on the front cover of the American version of *Are You Experienced*. That American edition would ultimately reach number five in the U.S. charts. It's doubtful that it would have climbed so high were it not for the stunning performance by the Experience at the Monterey International Pop Festival on June 18, 1967. The festival, the first of its kind in an age where jazz and blues had been the only forms of music deemed appropriate for such sprawling, star-studded events, took place from June 16 to 18. It was the recommendation of Paul McCartney that secured the Experience a slot—the band was unknown to most of the predominantly American festival organizers. In his performance on the third day, Hendrix became an overnight sensation in a country where he had not previously been able to muster anything but sideman work.

On the 18th, there was some disagreement backstage as to whether the Who or the Jimi Hendrix Experience should take the stage first. Both acts (then, incidentally, possessing the same nonentity status in America) were so explosive that it was feared it would be impossible for one to follow the other. According to a couple of witnesses—including Pete Townshend—a coin was flipped to decide. Hendrix lost, and was left facing the prospect of following the Who's invariably rousing, instrument-smashing finale. Chris Stamp, who was involved with both bands, was caught in the middle by the dispute, although he says, "In a real sense the Who were much more my artists than Jimi, because they were the band that we'd begun all this together." Stamp has a slightly different take on the argument: namely, that Hendrix didn't care who went first, but was nervous that the crowd would notice that he had lifted many of his stage tricks from the Who. "He just didn't want to go on *next* to the Who," he says, "so it was Jimi who went and said, 'They've got to change it.' He wasn't trying to do a tantrum. He knew that he'd stolen Pete Townshend's act. So he didn't want it to be that obvious. That's all."

The Grateful Dead was chosen to be a buffer between the Experience's and the Who's sets, and both U.K. bands went down like a storm. The Experience's set featured "Killing Floor," "Foxy Lady," "Like a Rolling Stone," "Rock Me Baby," "Hey Joe," "Can You See Me," "The Wind Cries Mary," "Purple Haze," and "Wild Thing." "He wanted to pull out all the stops," says Redding. "It was a hard job after the Who." Hendrix climaxed the proceedings by repeating the burning guitar stunt he'd used on the Walker Brothers tour. Stamp: "He was this unknown black American who'd gone to London and become this gigantic creative composer and musician, and his first gig back in his native land was this amazing moment. " Vic Briggs of the new Animals (the stars of the first night) was watching on closed circuit TV in the backstage club. "The Who seemed childish when they smashed their instruments," he opines. "It seemed petulant, it seemed pointless. It irritated me highly. When Jimi did his thing, there was something about it that was just enormously powerful and moving. It just grabbed me. I can't put it into words. It was so intense. He definitely tore the place apart. People went berserk after his thing. [The] Mamas and the Papas came on to follow it: it seemed like a big anti-climax to me." Redding concludes by stating, "It made the band in America."

June 28 saw the Experience take part in their first recording session outside the United Kingdom, entering TTG Studios in Hollywood to lay down the backing track for "The Stars That Play with Laughing Sam's Dice." On July 8, there started a series of concerts that were even more of a farcical mismatch of styles and audience demographics than the Walker Brothers tour had been: the Experience set off to traverse America with teenybopper idols the Monkees. There were good intentions behind the idea, however. Monkees drummer and lead singer Micky Dolenz had simply wanted to offer a helping hand to a musician he admired.

The second American Jimi Hendrix Experience single was released on August 16. Despite the Monterey triumph, "Purple Haze," backed by "The Wind Cries Mary," would only reach number 65. Although Scott McKenzie's hippie anthem "San Francisco (Be Sure to Wear Some Flowers in Your Hair)" and Jefferson Airplane's blatantly carnal "Somebody to Love" had recently graced the U.S. Top Ten, "Purple Haze" was just a little too wild at that time to secure mainstream radio play. What it did do, though, was serve as an ambassador, in all the important places, for the forthcoming U.S. release of the album. *Are You Experienced* appeared in America on Reprise on Wednesday, August 23, 1967, catalog number RS 6261. The album was quite different than its U.K. counterpart, to the dismay of many involved. Reprise had jettisoned "Red House," "Remember," and "Can You See Me" in favor of "Hey Joe," "Purple Haze" and "The Wind Cries Mary," and those tracks that were left from the U.K. release were jumbled. The only sensible change was the cover. Replacing the drab U.K. sleeve was a color fish-eyed shot from Karl Ferris's Kew Gardens shoot (with the Experience members in their best psychedelic gear) and some fashionably wild lettering.

Stamp was furious at Reprise's tampering with the track listing: "They did the very thing that Track was always saying, 'That's why we want to be an independent record label.' They did exactly the sort of bullshit that record companies do. He didn't have control over it. Jimi always related to Track. He would always come personally with his records to Track. And he always gave the masters to Track before Reprise."

Nevertheless, the record wowed the American critics and enchanted the American public, whose increasingly sophisticated tastes were illustrated by the fact that *Surrealistic Pillow* by Jefferson Airplane and the Doors' eponymous debut album were currently riding high in the charts (as, of course, was *Sgt. Pepper*). Significantly, *Are You Experienced* didn't need a hit single to make the American Top Five ("All Along the Watchtower" would be Hendrix's only U.S. Top Forty single). Although the Hendrix camp had cannily negotiated a promotional budget of $20,000 (then unheard of for a new artist), the Monterey splashdown, ecstatic word of mouth, and, perhaps most important, FM radio combined to make success in the singles medium irrelevant.

April of that year had seen the dawn of a revolution in American radio when San Francisco deejay Tom Donahue pioneered what became known as progressive radio: playing tracks simply because he liked them rather than because they were considered hit parade material. All over the United States, FM stations—whose superior audio fidelity had previously been the preserve of easy listening and classical music—began to adopt a format of playing album cuts by the likes of Bob Dylan, the Byrds, Ritchie Havens, the Paul Butterfield Blues Band, the Rolling Stones, Donovan, and the Beatles (especially the latter's more esoteric tracks). FM became known as the domain of classier, more adult-oriented music, and it was here that *Are You Experienced* found its niche. The album would spend 106 weeks on *Billboard*'s album chart, 77 of them in the Top Forty.

The age of the album artist was here. It's difficult to imagine a better album that could have ushered it in.

aftermath

WEIRD AS IT MAY SEEM CONSIDERING the multimillion-dollar industry his legacy constitutes, Jimi Hendrix released only two more studio albums in his lifetime. Before his tragic death in 1970, only *Axis: Bold As Love* and *Electric Ladyland* (both released in 1968) furthered the path so triumphantly begun with the Experience's debut. The live 1970 *Band of Gypsys* album was the last proper Hendrix release of his career.

Axis: Bold As Love was an album so distinctly different from *Are You Experienced* that it boggles the mind that its sessions continued on so seamlessly from the debut's. It was a collection of tracks that pushed the guitar virtuosity slightly into the background (although the album boasted some fantastic axemanship) and brought Hendrix's abilities as a composer (and poet) more to the fore: "Little Wing," "Castles Made of Sand," and "Wait Until Tomorrow" proved that Hendrix had as great a gift for melody as virtually any of his contemporaries, as well as an endearingly tender heart. Interestingly, many of those in and around Hendrix's circle cite this album as his masterpiece. "The first one is very exciting," says Noel Redding, "[but] I prefer *Axis: Bold As Love*. The songs. They're all just as good, and by which time we'd really progressed on our work in the studio. The first one was very raw. The second one was still raw, but refined.'" Roger Mayer and Lonnie Youngblood concur.

The double album *Electric Ladyland* was the release over which Hendrix had the most control. Now the de facto producer, he pursued any creative impulse and production idea he wanted to. The results were mixed. The deliciously brutal "Crosstown Traffic" and Hendrix's reimagining of Bob Dylan's "All Along the Watchtower" (a glorious coloring-in of Dylan's fine pencil sketch) were worthy additions to Hendrix's growing canon of classic recordings, but tracks such as the extremely lengthy superstar jam "Voodoo Chile" (which was not only average but, new for Hendrix music, patience-wearing) showed that being in complete control of one's art is not necessarily ideal. "I like fifty percent of it," says Redding. "I don't really like the tunes. 'A Merman I Would Be' and all that stuff—they're good songs and they're well done, but they wouldn't be for me."

In September 1968, having already quit as Hendrix's producer, Chandler divested himself of any management role in Hendrix's life, exasperated by Hendrix's increasing lack of discipline and his unsavory entourage, as well as by disputes with Jeffery. Mitchell and Redding were also becoming disillusioned. Hendrix's self-indulgence spilled over into his live work. "By 1968, it just got down to jamming blues onstage, and he wouldn't play any of the hits," Redding recalls. "I like playing blues, but I don't like playing blues all night." Redding and Mitchell staged a double resignation in the summer of 1969.

Band of Gypsys seemed to merely underline what a great rhythm section Hendrix had sacrificed. An album featuring the titular group that Hendrix had put together to play gigs for the purpose of recording a record that would pay off Ed Chalpin, it was a collection of flat, drab performances record-ed at the Fillmore East on New Year's Day 1970. The format was still a trio but, with Buddy Miles's drumming and Billy

Cox's bass playing, it was anything but a power trio. Even the title, the misspelling of which no one seems to have noticed, hints at an inertia surrounding the whole project. Chalpin, incidentally, seems not to be satisfied with the money he has made from this album. He recently told the media of his plan to release *Are You Experienced* on the resurrected Track label, thus forcing Universal Music—which now licenses Hendrix recordings from the Hendrix family—to enjoin him and subsequently be obliged to prove in court that Chalpin does not own the recording, thus neatly reversing the normal burden of proof. Chalpin is somewhat less forthcoming about the details of money withheld from the members of the Jimi Hendrix Experience by Mike Jeffery, whose estate Chalpin now administers.

The artistic decline of Hendrix was matched by a decline in his personal life. The growing realization that there was a disparity between what his records generated and what Mike Jeffery was paying him, his split with Kathy Etchingham, his artistic frustration, pressure on him from militant blacks to support a cause he didn't feel a particular affinity with, and various other pressures all took a toll. "I'd hear these stories of Jimi beating up women and smashing his hotel room to matchwood, and this wasn't the Jimi I knew," says Brian Auger in horror. "This was somebody else. The demons had really got to Jimi somehow or other." Hendrix's descent was brought fully home to the organist in 1970: "I was in New York and I got a call from John McLaughlin. We'd been friends for years. John said, 'You got to come down to the studio—I'm mixing my album, *Devotion*.'" When Auger arrived McLauglin wasn't in the building, but Alan Douglas,

McLauglin's producer and the man who would supervise several controversial posthumous Jimi Hendrix albums, was. "Before John got there, the door opened and in came Jimi with his girlfriend," Auger recalls. "I was very pleased to see him. Came up and gave me a hug. We were listening to the mix of this album for a bit, but I got kind of pissed off with the attitude of Alan Douglas and the engineer, who treated Jimi as if, 'Well this is the new guy on the block and you're done. It's all over for you. He's miles ahead of anything you can do.' To the point where I decided I didn't want to stay." When Auger left, Hendrix and his female companion followed him: "We got outside and I looked at Jimi and Jimi's skin was gray. He looked really gone. His girlfriend wasn't in very much better condition either. He opened this silver paper and snorted something. I think it was heroin. He looked at me and said, 'Oh I'm really sorry man—here . . . take a shot of this.' I said, 'Hey Jim—I don't do that stuff, man.' He said to me—this is something I'll never forget—'You know what, man? I need a lot more people 'round me like you.'"

"Nobody gave this man any advice for what would be good for him," opines Linda Keith, although she excludes Chandler from the criticism. "They gave him advice only for their own selfish requirement of him. And he went with it and it destroyed him. He was surrounded by dreadful, dreadful people." Etchingham, who fled Hendrix's circle when she found Hendrix to be associating with gun-toting narcotics dealers, says, "I think he was in a bit of a state of confusion towards the end. I don't think he knew which direction he was going in. I think he was being pulled by all kinds of sycophants this way and that way and befuddled by drugs and hangers-on. In retrospect, I can see the difference between the man that I first met and the one that died in 1970. It was enormous. He had aged ten years in four years."

Right up until his death, Hendrix never did seem to be able to settle on a new group of musicians. Stamp says, "I know that he understood that the Experience and that period of time in London and what happened there really had a sort of dynamic that he was never able to re-create. He kept trying to re-create it in a sense." Not that Stamp considers that the guitarist was completely adrift without the Experience: "He was basically using other musicians and different bands to try and elevate his writing skills and his recording skills and his musician skills. He was trying to go to a different place creatively." Nonetheless, one particular memory of Stamp's is poignant: "I watched a video quite late in Jimi's life of him—just some stuff I came across—and I played it to him and his face was just so lit up as he talked about Noel and Mitch, watching them: 'Oh, man—look at Mitch go!' He was so generous in his praise." Somewhat closer toward his death, Hendrix asked Redding to tour with him and Mitchell, who had rejoined the band. This was due to Billy Cox having fallen ill, but it's interesting to speculate what changes Hendrix may have made to his artistic plans when he found himself in the midst of that old Experience magic chemistry once more.

This planned reunion also seems interesting in light of Linda Keith's memory of Hendrix in his last months as a man trying to get back to simpler and happier times. Keith, who admits she felt a little proprietorial about the music of the man whose success had been a complete vindication of her belief in him, says that she and Hendrix would constantly argue about what she saw as his artistic downslide. "He'd parted from that complete symbiotic relationship with his guitar," she recalls. "It had changed by that time, whether it had become more an intellectual process or he was trying to do things that other people wanted him to do." Keith provided Hendrix a different perspective from that of the "sycophants" Etchingham refers to, though it wasn't appreciated: "I told him constantly. I don't think we ever had a conversation which didn't end in an argument. At that period I really didn't like him. Really gone off him." However, Keith detected that Hendrix knew she was right about one aspect of his decline: "He started to develop the triviality of his performance, because that's what always got the crowd screaming and I think that when he realized that the crowd would scream even when he was playing like shit, that upset him."

Keith believes that her message did at last start to get through to him. "He had this whole thing at the end of his life where he wanted to go back to how things were. He wanted to get back to that point of arriving in London." This applied to people from Hendrix's past as well as to his musical styles: "He'd been trying to get in touch with me at that time. I don't know if it was before or after the Isle of Wight, but I did see him for the last time in London and he was pretty upset with me." Keith was later touched to be told of a song Hendrix had written about her during this period. "Send My Love to Linda" has not yet made it onto an official release, but it is widely available among collectors. Keith feels the song underlines Hendrix's reflective mood shortly before his death.

On September 18, 1970, Hendrix died after taking a small

but fatal overdose of sleeping pills. Kathy Etchingham dismisses both conspiracy theories about his death (Mike Jeffery was reportedly getting very uptight about Hendrix's lack of co-operation regarding his business plans) and the suggestion that ambulance or hospital staff were negligent. Hendrix, according to Etchingham, would probably have survived if Monika Dannemann, his female companion of the day, had not told him the sleeping pills were very weak. Her subsequent claims that Hendrix died because he was strapped upright by incompetent ambulance staff were false. "What happened to Jimi is that he fell into the hands of a crazy fan, pure and simple," she says. "That's what did for him. He was in the wrong place at the wrong time with the wrong person. And she was a nutter. She proved herself to be a nutter and eventually killed herself."

Neither Noel Redding nor Mitch Mitchell ever joined a name band after Hendrix's death. Mitchell did overdubbing work on several posthumous Hendrix albums and is today involved with the Hendrix estate. Redding, less well connected, suffered years of hardship and harrowing legal headaches in an attempt to get his due royalties for Experience records. He is scathing about Jeffery. Of Stamp and Lambert, he says, "I never got a penny from Track Records. Nothing. And we sold a load of records." His suffering seemed to be at an end when the Hendrix family gained control of the guitarist's recordings in the 1990s. It was not to be: "I was told by Janie Hendrix that I was gonna get my artist's royalties, then I had this nasty legal letter about three or four months later saying they're going to uphold my settlement and I don't get nothing." Nonetheless, he says he is glad to have been a member of the Experience:

"It's still quite weird. I was in America a couple of months ago. I can't even go into a fucking supermarket without getting recognized. My girlfriend says I like it. I suppose I do like it."

Before his death, Hendrix had been working on the proper follow-up to *Electric Ladyland*. His working title was believed to be *First Rays of the New Rising Sun*. It took more than a quarter of a century for this album—or what is, in Hendrix's absence, its nearest approximation—to be issued. The tracks from it were instead initially distributed between posthumous releases including *The Cry of Love* and *Rainbow Bridge*, albums that, for all their disjointedness, were hailed as indications of what would have been Hendrix's artistic revival. That they were not was, ironically, proven by the 1997 CD release of *First Rays of the New Rising Sun*—"Angel" and "Belly Button Window" are sweet, but they are pale imitations of previous Hendrix ballads such as "Little Wing"; none of the rockers really take off, and there is a general absence of luster. More alarming, many of Hendrix's guitar solos are nothing less than boring. The album's tracks are better than both the songs and performances on *Band of Gypsys*, but the overall impression created is of a man bewildered by the fact that he is unable to come up with classics as he did in those effortlessly inspired sessions for *Are You Experienced*.

critical reactions

"IT HAS ABOUT THREE OR FOUR DIFFERENT MOODS," Jimi Hendrix said of *Are You Experienced* at the time of its release. "It has a little, you know, rock and roll . . . and then it . . . has a blues. Then it has a few freak-out tunes." A fair enough description of the album's contents—up to a point. Hendrix would, sadly, never know that more than three decades later—despite the hundreds of thousands of records issued in the interim—*Are You Experienced* would be still be among the best dozen albums ever made.

Not that it attracted universal praise at the time. *Rolling Stone*, for one, was unimpressed. Its clued-in reviewer had heard the U.K. edition and spent part of his review complaining that "Red House" wasn't present on the U.S. version. He stated that Hendrix was a "great guitarist and a brilliant arranger" but "neither a great songwriter nor an extraordinary vocalist." He criticized what he felt to be "the poor quality of the songs and the inanity of the lyrics." Although he had good things to say about "Purple Haze," "Hey Joe," "The Wind Cries Mary," and "I Don't Live Today," he concluded, "Above all this record is unrelentingly violent and, lyrically, inartistically violent at that."

Hendrix camp follower Keith Altham could be expected to take a more sympathetic stance in his analysis of the album for Britain's *New Musical Express*, and did so in a track-by-track description that was banal when it wasn't fawning. ("This is an incredible long track which leaves me wondering what the heck it's all about!" was his cringe-making description of "3rd Stone from the Sun.") There's no arguing with the accuracy of his summary, however, when he said, "The LP is a brave effort by Hendrix to produce a musical form which is original and exciting."

Melody Maker was impressed by the record's complete lack of commercial compromise and said of the Experience, "They thunder and charge along on some hammering tempos. They change speed mid-number; stop, start, fade, fizzle, simmer, and burn in a cauldron of beautiful fire. Hendrix is on roaring guitar form . . . with some extremely atmospheric organic sounds which have an uncanny knack of circling through your mind and blowing the top of your head off."

This type of slack-jawed reaction to the album has faded slightly over the years as the record's novelty has worn off, but the aesthetic esteem in which *Are You Experienced* is held has actually deepened. Chris Welch—who has the dual distinction of having written both the first Hendrix live review to appear in the U.K. press and the first book-length Hendrix biography—says that, to him, the album is as powerful now as it was in 1967. "It created a big shock then," he says. "It still creates a shock listening to it again. It still sounds amazingly fresh and exciting. There's no music being made like that now, certainly not in that spontaneous kind of way. It's that spontaneity and interplay between Noel, Mitch, and Jimi that makes it dynamic." In addition to the album's sonic power is its eclecticism: "Every track has a different feel. You can hear funk and soul in 'Fire' and psychedelic in '3rd Stone from the Sun' and pure blues in 'Red House.' 'May This Be Love,' which has a got a Latin feeling to it, that's quite unpredictable. Each track has a different personality to it."

Charles Shaar Murray was a 16-year-old schoolboy when he first heard *Are You Experienced*. "I knew instantly it was a totally miraculous record," he recalls. "Absolutely outstanding. I just remember listening to it and thinking, 'Oh my God—what is *that?*'" When Murray became a rock critic—a career choice that would see him publish the acclaimed 1989 Hendrix critique *Crosstown Traffic*—and had the time and means to study popular music more deeply, he became even more impressed by the album: "What it took me years to realize is that, technologically speaking, it was done with very restricted means. When you break most of it down, it's just a trio performance with a lead guitar overdub, basically. And it wasn't done with incredibly advanced technology or studio facilities at all, but the reason it sounded so extraordinary is the actual performances and the imagination of Hendrix and Chandler. They didn't have anything like the amount of time and money and gadgetry that the Beatles had to make *Sgt. Pepper*."

Dave Marsh wrote the liner notes to the 1997 CD reissue of *Are You Experienced* and gave evidence for the Hendrix family in the court case which led to them acquiring the rights to Hendrix's music. In said liner notes he states that *Are You Experienced* is nothing less than the greatest debut album of all time. "I meant what I said," he says simply. "You know: I thought about it." Murray—while tipping his hat to the first albums of the likes of the Doors, the Velvet Underground, the Patti Smith Group, and the Clash—can't find it in his heart to reject Marsh's ranking of *Are You Experienced*: "All those albums are monumental. I would say at the very least it's in there and stands comparison with all of them, but if I wanted to go out on a limb, that would be a pretty good limb to go out on."

Not that the record is considered by anyone to be flawless. "'Fire' I think dates badly," says Marsh. "That's very psyche-delic and very of the period. And 'Foxy Lady,' as powerful as it is, it's really hampered by the language he uses. It's like Marvin Gaye's 'Let's Get It On.' Don't listen to the lyrics too long, because you'll be reminded that that was then, this is now. You couldn't get over in a bar with 'Let's Get It On' now. It's just corny. Who would say that to someone now?" For his part, Chris Welch feels that the album succeeds in spite of, not because of, the rawness of its sound quality: "It's that strange sort of sound compared to modern recordings." He also has reservations about the title track: "It's rather monoto-nous. It's still exciting and interesting to hear and it's got a par-ticularly powerful guitar introduction, but it sounds a bit doomy. There's that kind of marching rhythm to it as well." Murray is probably the kindest of the three critics regarding the album's shortcomings: "I wouldn't describe anything on it as weak. There are a few throwaways, but even the throw-aways are wonderful. I like 'Remember': it's the greatest Otis Redding B-side that never was. Even the lighthearted, com-paratively lightweight throwaways are magnificent, and each one is another little quadrant of Hendrix's musical universe."

As for the strongest tracks, Murray says, "I love 'Red House' because it was his first major blues. '3rd Stone from the Sun'—complete science fiction wonderland, a Trekkie on acid. The intro to the title track anticipated scratching by ten or fifteen years. 'Manic Depression'—a heavy metal blues waltz. Once I start listing highlights on this album, I could just go through it and end up naming nearly every track for one reason or another." Welch concurs about "Red House": "That is such a commanding treatment of the blues. If any other band had played that particular number it would sound like yet another turgid 12-bar blues. It brings the blues back to life."

Marsh is broadly happy with the American configuration of the album, which for many years was the only version he—like so many of his countrymen—knew. "I'm a singles guy," he shrugs. "I always think the singles belong on the album. I know that's a very American way to think." He does add, however: "If 'Red House' had been on the record, I would have liked the record more. I'd trade the other two [left off] for 'Purple Haze' and 'Hey Joe' any time, but I'd really like to have 'Red House' because that's sort of ground zero for his music and that's where it becomes apparent that he really is, on top of everything else, a Muddy Waters acolyte." Marsh cites "Purple Haze" and "I Don't Live Today" as the tracks he liked most when he first owned the album. "It was later on for me the complexity of '3rd Stone from the Sun' leapt out at me. I didn't hear until I had a bigger stereo what was going on towards the end of the record."

Welch, Murray, and Marsh do not feel that the record is particularly dated, partly because the psychedelic gimmicks of the time—backward guitar, speaker panning, and "far out" lexicon—are used relatively sparingly. Murray: "There's a lot of music from that era, a lot of psychedelic music, that does sound dated to the point of being kitsch." For him, *Are You Experienced* avoids these pitfalls because of "the rawness of the performance and the fact that the sound of well-recorded guitar, bass, and drums are pretty much timeless. There's nothing so dated as last year's drum machine." Marsh adds, "If people are going to go around praising Radiohead, then it hasn't dated a bit."

Another point of agreement for the three is the massive influence *Are You Experienced* has had on popular music. Marsh: "Part of it is just the whole guitar attack that people adopted afterwards. People were more interested in, and less afraid of, using devices that they would have thought of as completely gimmicky. Then you've got what I think happened to some degree with the way that the sound of bands like the Who and Cream actually evolved. Even Zappa. Although Frank generally followed his own star, I think that Hendrix opened some doors for him, as a guitarist as much as a composer. And then of course all the metal stuff. From Black Sabbath forward, every heavy metal band owes its gimlet heart to Hendrix."

Of Hendrix's influence on metal bands, Murray says, "What they picked up on were the most superficial aspects of Hendrix. But for a long time, when Hendrix's critical stock was low, it was the heavy metal guys more than anybody else who still kept him on a pedestal." Murray also mentions the Who and Cream as artists who realized they would have to buck up their ideas to keep step with Hendrix, but he is anxious to point out that it wasn't merely rock or pop artists who were affected: "You have to remember the influence that he had on the likes of George Clinton, the influence he had on Miles Davis. Hendrix had a fundamental effect on soul music and jazz and certain areas of blues."

Welch (who posits Robin Trower as an obvious disciple of

Hendrix) makes the point that the album's effect may even have extended beyond music: "I wonder how long-term the influence of that album was, maybe on people we don't even know about, like, say, film directors or writers. Lots of people who would have had their ideas changed around, opened up, by that album. Listening to the very stoned, psychedelic sections of it it paints pictures in the mind a bit, and I imagine that could have influenced lots of artistic people in lots of ways."

Murray says he wrote *Crosstown Traffic* when he felt Hendrix's reputation was in decline to refute the idea that he was merely psychedelic kitsch or an early heavy metal player. He is now pleased at what he perceives as a turnaround that sees Hendrix revered as a great artist once more. Though he dismisses the theory of Hendrix's career as one marking an incremental decline as "bollocks," he is willing to concede the point that *Are You Experienced* was the most important album of Hendrix's career for both Hendrix and his listeners: "The drastic expansion of the sonic palette," is how he sums up the effect of *Are You Experienced*. "Completely changed notions of what a guitar could sound like, or indeed, what music could sound like." He adds, "It was classically psychedelic in that it was mind-expanding. It was a wake-up call for the collective imagination."

the songs

Foxy Lady

(Appears on the U.K. and U.S. versions)

The U.K. version of *Are You Experienced* has the perfect album opening: the sound of Hendrix scraping his pick down a string to produce the effect of his guitar emerging from the aural distance, gradually increasing in volume and then exploding—with a flare of feedback—into "Foxy Lady"'s sublimely lecherous riff.

Hendrix's riff is not the staccato work that is beloved by heavy metallers, but one that utilizes the qualities made possible by his cranked-up amps to create a delightfully rippling and continuous sound. Furthermore, Hendrix enriches even that unusually exotic palette by throwing in the occasional flourish, the bright, trebly, solid-bodied sonic qualities of which are a deliciously startling contrast to those of that thin, growling lick.

An additional contrast to the type of heavy metal with which Hendrix's music is, ludicrously, so often associated is the sweetness of his manner and sentiments. "Foxy Lady" is without doubt a song about sex. Decades of rock singers' braggadocio has made us automatically assume that speaking or singing about sex equates with boastfulness or oppressiveness. To celebrate the pleasures of intercourse is a perfectly natural human desire, for both men and women. "Foxy Lady" does precisely and merely that—and when Hendrix sings "I'm coming to git ya," he is being playful, not predatory.

The absence of "Wild Thing" on this album might very well be explained by this opening track. Surely, "Foxy Lady" is Hendrix's rewriting of that Chip Taylor classic. Though there is no direct plagiarism, the common attributes of the two songs are so significant as to seem to rule out coincidence. "Wild Thing" and "Foxy Lady" are both compositions with a great blaring dirty riff, a stop-start structure, and an unashamedly horny ambience.

Manic Depression

(Appears on the U.K. and U.S. versions)

"Manic Depression" is the finest example of the excellence of the Experience as a group and the ultimate proof of the idiocy of the opinions of the likes of Nik Cohn. On "Manic Depression," all three members of the Jimi Hendrix Experience are operating as equals. Hendrix's playing is of the elevated nature one takes for granted with him, but the rhythm section is on fire. Mitchell's drums are heart-stopping in both their thunder and their relentlessness. Redding's playing, meanwhile, is sublime: when Hendrix pauses each time before singing the line about what manic depression is doing to him (effectively the chorus of the song), Redding shatters the silence with brawny, climbing basslines that are utterly fabulous.

Those who thought "Purple Haze" was pushing the envelope in terms of volume, distortion, and sheer musical belligerence must have been astounded that, on this track, not only was the Experience able to go further in all of those areas, but actually went considerably further. "Manic Depression" is brutally aggressive and colossally loud. It never lets up in its determination to make as much noise as possible: even those pauses before the title refrain vocal line are splintered by an unyielding Redding. Nothing—not the Velvet Underground's clangorous experimentation on its first album (released a couple of months before the release of *Are You Experienced*), not Dave Davies's amp-shredding performance on "You Really Got Me" in 1964—had ever sounded this extreme before.

And yet, the song at no point threatens to become unlistenable. A keen musicality is evident at every juncture. The Experience may not have sat down and plotted each counterpoint and contrast—they weren't that kind of band—but the song is superbly structured. Instruments drop away and inflections are introduced in an intricate arrangement that is the antithesis of a featureless aural assault. In addition to the contrasts within the instrumentation is the extreme counterpoint the lyric (and the melody it rides on) provides to the artillery shell music. "Manic Depression" is not the song of self-assertion implied by its music. Its words are insecure ruminations, frequently almost muttered by Hendrix. At the ends of verses, Hendrix's voice rises climatically (something required by the swelling melody line), but by the beginning of the next verse is back to a mumbled hesitancy, appropriately mirroring the way somebody in the emotional doldrums will determine to do something to improve his situation and then deflate in a confidence-draining second.

As the song careens toward a close, Hendrix and Mitchell indulge in a bout of call and response, throwing the gauntlet of sonic outrage back and forth to each other. Then Hendrix signals that it's time to bring proceedings to a finish with a note on the guitar that is just a little too earsplitting and distorted to be called keening. Mitchell takes the cue with some climatic kit explorations, while Hendrix brings the song home with incrementally descending single notes. The track ends in a gentle rush of feedback and exhausted cymbal splashes.

Red House

(Appears on the U.K. version)

The 12-bar "Red House" succeeds artistically precisely because it makes a mockery of the blues' limitations. Blues is boring. This opinion may outrage many, but a musical genre that relies for differentiation on new lyrics over an interchangeable musical format (many of which lyrics are permutations of the same stock phrases) is so limited in scope as to be farcical.

In "Red House," Hendrix crams into the blues more than was ever meant to go. The reliably stately pace of typical blues music is shredded by Hendrix, who peels off tidal waves of notes, cramming ever greater and faster runs between every second line (and doing so with a guitar that is cranked up so high that it creates a mental image of an instrument as big as the titular house). Before long, Hendrix's determination to cram in the longest and most complicated fretboard explorations possible in the few seconds before the first bar of the next line looms becomes so exhilarating as to be comedic. One wants to laugh out loud at Hendrix's audacity. The hilarity factor is only increased by the preposterous disparity between his ultramodern, quicksilver virtuosity and the sheer generic mediocrity of the plodding, bog-standard twelve-bar pattern that Redding and Mitchell maintain behind him. (This is not intended as a slight on Hendrix's colleagues—it is the blues that is mediocre, not them.) It is as though Hendrix's swooping, soaring, whooping guitar lines are scrawling graffiti over an undeservedly venerated old painting. To this critic, Hendrix's guitar playing on this track is the greatest of his career. He may have shown greater sonic innovation on recordings such as "Purple Haze," but for technical brilliance and breathtaking mellifluousness, he never topped "Red House." Some might use pejoratives such as showboating or flashy to describe it, but since when have showboats restricted themselves to less than four minutes?

Though a lyric that is required by convention to repeat the first line of each verse is naturally limited in its scope, even here Hendrix throws in the odd little touch that reveals he is better than the form. For instance, most blues writers would have said that they hadn't seen their baby in, for example, "oh so many days." That Hendrix comes out with "99 and one-half days" is the sort of clever little twist that keeps the lyric cruising clear of cliché.

Those who have concluded from this track, however, that Hendrix was deliberately mocking the blues were—sadly—wrong. On stage, Hendrix was inclined to perform twenty-minute versions of the number. The very tension between the plodding and the manic that made the *Are You Experienced* version of "Red House" so great simply didn't exist in flabby and interminable live renditions. Hendrix wasn't making fun of the blues, after all—he was in fact absurdly respectful of it—and the brilliance of the song as it appears on *Are You Experienced* was merely a happy accident created by Hendrix's adherence, at the time, to the concept of short playing times. This doesn't detract from the sublimeness of the original, but it is disappointing to realize that, in this respect at least, Hendrix wasn't quite as clever as he seemed.

Can You See Me

(Appears on the U.K. version)

"Can You See Me" is a track with a dark and slightly menacing atmosphere. For the first time on the album, Hendrix ain't no nice guy. Here he is dismissive about the idea that a lover who has recently walked out on him is worth begging to. There is a grimness of tone, with none of the playfulness and uncertainty evident in Hendrix's voice in the album's first three tracks (although the concluding verse reveals that he still wants the lover to return to him). The double tracking of Hendrix's defiant vocal only adds to the unyielding tone. The song is given a tinge of the surreal by the metaphors used: if the woman can see the narrator begging her on his knees, she can see a thousand years into the future.

The music is of a piece with the words. For large parts of the song all three members of the band play a piston-regular riff in synchronization, making it seem as if they are hammering home the lyric's message of no compromise. As with much of Hendrix's music, it's difficult to identify what part of Hendrix's playing constitutes the song's riff. There are several different guitar parts that fit the bill of a hook, ranging from a simple four-note pattern to an elongated, ferocious metallic strum, to an overdubbed, echoing, and exotic-sounding progression: hook is piled densely upon hook, with parts interlocking so naturally as to make the distinction between rhythm and lead playing meaningless.

The track has a surprise ending. Through its stop-starts, the song's tension builds as it continues, each reentry by the musicians after the silent pauses progressively more intense. Yet, just when a cacophonous and denunciatory climax is expected, the song ends in a final dismissive comment from Hendrix and an untidy clatter and burp of instrumentation, as though everybody has suddenly lost interest. It works: the very uninterest and carelessness of the close is perfectly in keeping with the don't-give-a-damn tone of the track.

Love or Confusion

(*Appears on the U.K. and U.S. versions*)

"Love or Confusion" is the first track on *Are You Experienced* that is not built upon recognizable musical foundations. Although the songs hitherto have all been experimental in their own ways, this composition is almost otherworldly in its unusualness. Its departure from the preceding tracks is almost jarringly apparent from the first note: a trebly single guitar strum, which is followed by some bass work from Redding that is disconcertingly reminiscent of a human pulse, followed by the introduction of drumming mixed in such a way as to make Mitchell sound as though he is far off in the distance, yet still clearly audible. The surreal and exotic feel is then deepened by Hendrix's subsequent guitar work: it's as though not guitar notes, but sparkles and comet flares are dancing before us. To cap it all, when Hendrix starts singing, he sounds as if he is standing atop a mountain overlooking a canyon of which we, the listeners, are at the bottom, his words traveling down to us through a series of echoes.

It doesn't stop there. The track is an incredibly heady concoction of variations of color and texture: undulating guitar parts—all with different tones—overlap and interlock and separate again. One guitar part provides a quiet howl of feedback at regular junctures and, miraculously, sounds no less musical than the track's conventional guitar work. When an interlude occurs, up pops another amazing part: a scraped guitar string, whose quiet, continuous rasping quality is like some kind of small engine warming up. Mitchell's circular drumming patterns echo Hendrix's lyric, which refers to the narrator's mind going 'round and 'round as he tries to solve the puzzle about the mental state expressed in the song's title. The mundanity of such a dilemma is undermined by the fact that Hendrix is referring to such things as reaching up and touching the sun. Behind everything, there is Redding who—every time he becomes audible—is contributing that very slightly disquieting pulsing.

This track is not just a song, it is an aural painting. Everything in it is used to color and shade and provide perspective (and then make nonsense of perspective). It's a triumph not only for the group, but for the producer and engineer. And yet, though it is obviously a track that simply could not have been made without modern-day electric instruments and cutting-edge studio technology, there is something about "Love or Confusion" that seems utterly ancient. How mind-blowing all this must have been to the audience of 1967.

I Don't Live Today

(*Appears on the U.K. and U.S. versions*)

No one, absolutely no one, could have maintained the sheer staggering brilliance of this album's first five tracks, so it would be absurd to be disappointed or surprised that the following song, "I Don't Live Today" (the last track on side one of the original vinyl release) constitutes a slight falling away of quality.

Inevitably, there are several good things about this track. Hendrix's lyric—which from comments he subsequently made seems to be concerned with the plight of the American Indians—is excellent. When he says he wishes that somebody would hurry up and rescue him so that he can be on his "miserable way," he is superbly, and with great economy of words, evoking despair, whether that despair be an individual's or the despair of a devastated and brutalized race. There are several sublime musical elements, too. Hendrix's guitar break has a nice liquidy quality to it. Mitchell's drumming is, as ever, never less than thoroughly imaginative. His dropped beats create a pleasantly disorienting lag effect. When he resumes a normal signature as he moves with Hendrix into the instrumental break, his drumming matches Hendrix's guitar work for gorgeous fluidity.

Yet the bad outweighs the good. Hendrix always had a masterful ability to make a brutal riff sound attractive, "Purple Haze" being the classic example. Yet the six-note lick on "I Don't Live Today" fails to delight in the same way. Its unimaginativeness is the very opposite of the incredible sonic invention of "Purple Haze," and the lick's repetition almost becomes irritating. What sinks the track ultimately is the feedback. The way that the wails of Hendrix's cranked-up guitar rush into the listener's face is presented as interesting in its own right, yet Hendrix doesn't do anything clever with it as he does on the previous track, nor does he incorporate it into the melody or arrangement. The track ends up as frequently formless and often comes perilously close to being a din.

May This Be Love

(Appears on the U.K. and U.S. versions)

The otherworldly, keening guitar sounds that follow "I Don't Live Today" lead the listener to expect this to be another "weird" track. In fact, we get a more or less conventional ballad, with instrumentation as stark as its message of devotion is simple. Though the choice of a gentle ballad to kick off what was originally side 2 of *Are You Experienced* (as indeed it appears on the U.K. version) is peculiar, "May This Be Love" is a wonderful song. Other than "The Wind Cries Mary," it would be the first proof to listeners of the time that there was a sentimental and a melodic side to the so-called Wild Man of Borneo.

The song has a slightly Eastern feel in the verses, with Hendrix singing sweetly and delicately over exotic guitar lines. Where Hendrix's guitar is not Eastern it is aquatic. Mitchell's restrained patterns add to the atmosphere. This air is dramatically dispensed with in the middle eight when, after a pause, the band launches briefly into a rising and raunchy rock style. The entire instrumental break is lengthy and lovely, with Hendrix's guitar line swooping and dipping like a graceful bird in flight. The mono mix of the album may be viewed as superior by some, but the way the guitar and drums pan back and forth between speakers during the instrumental break in the stereo edition only adds to this song's delightfulness.

Fire

(Appears on the U.K. and U.S. versions)

Although it may have been inspired by the heating arrangements at her home, Noel Redding's mother surely couldn't have imagined that she would be responsible for the genesis of an expression of such carnal yearning as "Fire." Hendrix's beseechment of a woman to let him stand next to her fire is, when one thinks about it, a not completely logical metaphor for sexual congress. As with a lot of vaguely silly ideas in rock, however, it becomes something one is prepared to make allowances for—even embrace—because of the quality of the musical frame in which it is set. This particular frame is fabulous, not least because of Mitch Mitchell.

"Fire" is surely Mitch Mitchell's finest hour. Excellent as Hendrix's concept is, infectious as is the enthusiasm of his singing, and nicely melodramatic as Redding's basslines are, it is Mitchell's absolutely pitiless playing that lifts the song into the realms of the classic. He simply never stops. Mitchell's relentlessness, however, is not the monotonous pounding on the snare drum to which most drummers would resort in order to attempt to create intensity. Instead, he comes up with a series of ferocious, circular, and hand-blur-ringly fast patterns. Even when he is given a solo, he maintains proportion and imagination. The song does have the requisite guitar break (to which the singer's "Move over Rover—and let Jimi take over!" is a delightful way-paver), but it's shorter than one might expect and is followed by a second vocal-less interlude in which the spotlight is handed to Mitchell, as though Hendrix and Redding were so amazed at their colleague's brilliance that they felt compelled to spontaneously drop a guitar part and just let the listener enjoy his playing. Mitchell rises to the occasion not with hackneyed paradiddles, but with some relaxed playing that uses silences for effect as much as it employs muscle.

3rd Stone from the Sun

(Appears on the U.K. and U.S. versions)

At half of its length, "3rd Stone from the Sun" would have been a very good, dreamy instrumental interlude before the album's punchier remainder. The song is fatally weakened, however—and the entire album sustains a flesh wound—because it not only outstays its welcome but, in that extraneous playing time, mistakes technical innovation for aesthetic worth.

The track starts out well, like a Shadows instrumental brought into the space age: just as Hank Marvin explored the possibilities of lead guitar lines on the Stratocaster, presenting lines that were interesting in their own right—not just scene-setting for a vocal—on hits such as "Apache" and "FBI," so does Hendrix in the first couple of minutes of "3rd Stone . . . ." Redding's bass commands equal attention: the melody he is playing bears no relation to that of the guitar, thus presenting an alternative option in the unlikely event that some might not want to listen to Hendrix's fretwork. Then things begin to go wrong. As though the two are trying to cancel out the qualities of their playing for the first few minutes, Redding's bass figures become repetitive and overly simple, and Hendrix's feedback and backward experiments lose sight of the first standard of music: listenability. The listenability factor is also affected by the fact that—unthinkable on all other tracks—one looks at one's watch. Because the soporific nature of "3rd Stone . . ." couldn't be a more unfortunate contrast to the way that every other song crackles and bristles with energy, it results in a profound slowing of the album's momentum. This might have been redeemed at the time by the novelty of the noises Hendrix was making, but 35 years later we are left with a boring period piece.

Remember

(Appears on the U.K. version)

Following "3rd Stone . . ." as it does (on the U.K. version of the album, at any rate), the conventionality of "Remember" is thoroughly refreshing, although it's not only by comparison that this song triumphs. "Remember" is a ludicrously under-rated song in the Hendrix canon. Yes, it is an R & B number (although had the word been more common then it would have been labeled soul) that lovingly embraces all the traditions of that genre—from its strident melody to its punchy rhythm to its use of the mockingbird motif—but it is in no way pedestrian. Hendrix delights in the traditions of the type of song he had once played night after night on the chitlin circuit, but he does so with the aid of a superb backing band and his own inimitable inventiveness. These make all the difference. The melody is simply delicious and makes for a wonderfully fresh and exuberant sound. That, and a lyric that holds out hope in the face of desertion, results in a track that, like many great love songs, has a sunny and life-affirming quality despite its sad tale. Of course, it's Hendrix's guitar playing that also lifts the track above the merely generic: those distinctive Hendrix qualities of quicksilver patterns and colossal volume serve to make of the form something that is grander and more resplendent, as though the genre has been dressed up in sonic ruffles and bows. The only black mark is a minor one: after Hendrix says that before his baby left him his mockingbird used to sing so "sweet," shouldn't the next line end with "week" rather than the non-rhyming "day"?

One should be suspicious of Hendrix fans who dismiss the likes of "Remember." Not only do their views have the smack of a self-conscious radicalism, they also betray a lack of understanding of both Hendrix the musician and Hendrix the man: "Remember" is no less quintessentially Hendrix than "Purple Haze."

Are You Experienced

(Appears on the U.K. and U.S. versions)

The placing of "Remember" (in the U.K. album version) in front of the album's title and closing track neatly—and startlingly—shows just far Jimi Hendrix had come in the space of less than a year. If "Remember" represents Hendrix's roots, "Are You Experienced" demonstrates how he built upon those roots to take his music into the stratosphere. "Remember"—and all the songs like it that Hendrix had performed in 101 dim and dank venues on the chitlin circuit—is performance. "Are You Experienced" is creation: the use of instruments to paint an aural picture. Integral to this is the obtaining from those instruments not their expected sounds, but the sounds you would least expect—and integral to that are production effects.

The track fades in. A fluttering backward guitar part (sounding uncannily like modern-day deejay scratching techniques) provides a fanfare for spangled guitar work and a very heavy percussive track. Hendrix's vocal, which occurs almost immediately, is both intimate (he's speaking in the second person) and distant (he doesn't waste time with formalities as he begins to almost hector the listener). Hendrix is encouraging the listener to become an initiate. Of what, however, is unclear. He could, of course, easily be talking about drugs (although he provides room for ambiguity with the final line: "Not necessarily stoned, but beautiful . . .") or, just as easily, he could be referring to sex. Then again, the song might be meaningless—the result of a whimsical desire to provide a sort of theme tune for a band called the Experience. It's irrelevant: both the lyric and the music are impressionistic. Shimmering strands of interweaving sounds in various degrees of focus dance across the rhythmic backdrop of shuffling backward rhythm guitar and quasi-militaristic drumming. The wheezing, fluttering backward guitar solo is truly stunning and clearly well thought out: the arbitrary sequences of noise that usually resulted from the tactic in this era would not have been so easy on the ear.

Whatever its considerable qualities, however, the album could have done with a less fey closer—something with more of an impact than this musical equivalent of a view through a kaleidoscope.

Hey Joe

(Appears on the U.S. version)

"Hey Joe" sounds unlike anything else in Hendrix's canon, but, to the credit of the band (and Chandler) seems anything but the flag of convenience and foot-in-the-door tactic it was. In his rendition of Billy Roberts' tragedy (filtered through Tim Rose's vision), Hendrix manages a remarkable feat: to create the definitive reading of a song that anybody and everybody (a lot of them supremely talented) had already tackled.

Strangely, the opening guitar figure and the rest of the song are almost like two unmatching components: the intro is so sudden, dramatic, and dagger-sharp, it makes one expect something altogether more searing and uptempo than the downbeat affair that follows. It's no matter, though, for the subsequent performance is exquisite in its brooding atmosphere and mood of defiance. Mitchell deserves much of the credit here. He adroitly sidesteps the problems many drummers face as to what to play on slow songs, crashing about his kit but doing it with such care and intelligence as to not destroy the mood in any way. Conceptually, the track's ending is magnificent (if probably unintended): Hendrix saying that no hangman is going to put a noose around his neck as the track is faded out paints a picture of a man disappearing into the distance—utterly apposite for a protagonist on the run. Hendrix's singing here and every-where else on the track would be impressive in any case, but knowing how shy and insecure he was about his vocals then, his passion and presence takes on another dimension.

Purple Haze

(Appears on the U.S. version)

"Purple Haze" was as great a departure from Hendrix's debut as could possibly be imagined. "Hey Joe" is, in terms of both theme and musical style, gritty reality. "Purple Haze" drives a coach and horses through the very concept of reality. The first bars are lumbering, dinosaur footsteps. Then the dinosaur speaks in the form of a gargantuan, growling riff, with Mitchell shadowing it for emphasis. The riff moves seamlessly into a swinging rhythm guitar part, the type of which Hendrix specialized in at the time: a supple, melodic, multiple-stringed affair—with outer margins blurred by distortion—that is far removed from the stabbed rhythm guitar style common at the time, yet avoids the equally unimaginative wall-of-sound rhythm guitar that is fashionable nowadays.

The lyric—whose rendition is EQed to make it sound like Hendrix is declaiming from Mars—is genuinely poetic and clever. Overfamiliarity has dulled us to its charms, but just think about that frisson of delight you experienced the first time you heard Hendrix say—in an insane aside to the listener—"'Scuse me while I kiss the sky!" The guitar solo is a stream of molten gold followed by some heavy breathing and the repetition of that growling riff once more. Another verse of grand-scale bewilderment—the protagonist, rather than not knowing what day of the week it is, is instead confused as to whether the timespace he occupies is tomorrow or the end of time—and soon we reach the end of the song, a fade where the molten gold guitar tone, counterpointed by some fine rocket-ship-engine bass, once again reigns.

The Wind Cries Mary

(*Appears on the U.S. version*)

"The Wind Cries Mary" boasts probably Hendrix's finest lyric. All the studying at the feet of Bob Dylan came together in a track that could pass for the missing verses of "Desolation Row." The two lines that counterpoint a queen weeping and a king having no wife are the high points of a song that is packed with dazzling imagery.

The music, however, is not as beautiful as the words—at

least, if one hears it in stereo. This author remains unconvinced of the claims for the superiority of the mono versions of *Are You Experienced* tracks, but without doubt ". . . Mary" gains power in that mix. Hendrix's guitar playing is a rather rude presence in stereo—emphasizing how his three-note descending part at the end of each verse is unimaginative by his standards—but in mono, everything slips into focus, especially his lovely, warm singing. The music is a little too stiff, unfortunately. Improvisation generally worked for the Experience, but here, the lack of suppleness inherent in first takes is just a little too evident.

The American version of *Are You Experienced* has its merits, despite the philistine motives of its compilers. After all, the inclusion of material such as "Hey Joe," "Purple Haze," and "The Wind Cries Mary" is hardly going to weaken an album, even if the exclusion of the incandescently great "Red House" is knuckleheaded. An album conceived as an organic entity by the artist should, however, have been respected and left intact.

One can argue forever over whether the U.K. or the U.S. version is the superior one. One could even throw another argument into the pot and say that contemporaneous B-sides "51st Anniversary" and "Highway Chile" would have made fine album tracks. The fact is that new technology and a changed consumer mentality have rendered it all academic: the age of CD has given us the capacity to have our cake and eat it, with running times that allow for all of the songs that appeared on both original releases to be contained in a single disc—which is exactly what MCA and the Hendrix family have done with the 1997 American and international reissues. It's difficult to avoid the conclusion that those reissues will now become the definitive editions of the album in the public's mind, and that in a generation's time people will barely be able to remember the original vinyl configurations. By then, the entire concept of the "authentic" contents of albums of the Experience's generation of artist might well be meaningless, and the universal employment of bonus tracks could mean that the purpose of an album from Hendrix's era will have become nothing more than a snapshot of where the artist was at that particular stage of his career. The 1997 reissues of the album—all the songs the Experience released from the sessions preceding the release of *Are You Experienced*—constitute just such a snapshot. Instead of worrying about purity or lack of organicness, we should just sit back and enjoy the music. It is an album that even today is an embarrassment of riches and, although "3rd Stone from the Sun" has its longueurs, there is not an unequivocal dud on it.

As stated in the introduction, *Are You Experienced* is clearly one of the greatest albums ever made.

acknowledgments

I would like to thank the following people for granting me interviews: Keith Altham, Brian Auger, Vic Briggs, George Chkiantz, Roger Daltrey, Micky Dolenz, Kathy Etchingham, Philip José Farmer, Bruce Fleming, Linda Keith, Dave Marsh, Jim Marshall, Roger Mayer, Charles Shaar Murray, Andrew Loog Oldham, Noel Redding, Mike Ross-Trevor, Chris Stamp, Seymour Stein, John Steel, Gerd Syllwasschy, Chris Welch, and Lonnie Youngblood.

My additional thanks go to Vic Briggs (also known as Antion Meredith) for reading the manuscript and making suggestions and corrections, as well as e-mailing me comments about the use of the tremolo arm, American FM radio, and his memories of the 1960s U.K. studio scene, which in places I have reproduced verbatim, and to George Chkiantz for patiently going over passages with me until my descriptions of recording techniques were something other than gibberish.

Chris Charlesworth, Tony Fletcher, and Richie Unterberger all very kindly supplied me with contact information and advice.

I am also indebted to the following Jimi Hendrix fans who helped me with the checking of facts on Hendrix bulletin boards: Doug Bell, Electric Henk, and Bill Scully.

Gary Geldeart, Steve Rodham, and Malcolm Stewart of the Hendrix fan magazine *Jimpress* provided invaluable help in the form of CDs, cuttings, advice, and query answering. Those who wish to see their very professional magazine and painstakingly researched books should contact them at

P.O. Box 218, Warrington, Cheshire, WA5 2FG, England. (E-mail: sr@jimpress.u-net.com; Web site: www.u-net.com/ ~jimpress).

Caesar Glebbeek, editor of the similarly professional Hendrix magazine *Univibes*, was also the source of contact information and invaluable help. *Univibes* is available from Coppeen, Enniskeane, Co. Cork, Republic of Ireland. E-mail: univibes@indigo.ie; Web site: www.univibes.com.

The following books on Jimi Hendrix all provided, to a greater or lesser degree, valuable facts and background information (the publication dates refer to the edition I personally made use of):

Are You Experienced by Noel Redding & Carol Appleby (Da Capo Press, New York, 1996)

The Complete Guide to the Music of Jimi Hendrix by John Robertson (Omnibus Press, London, 1995)

Crosstown Traffic by Charles Shaar Murray (Faber, London, 1989)

Eyewitness Hendrix by Johnny Black (Carlton, London, 1999)

From the Benjamin Franklin Studios by Gary Geldeart & Steve Rodham (Jimpress, Warrington, 1998)

Hendrix: A Biography by Chris Welch (Omnibus Press, London, 1982)

Hendrix: Setting the Record Straight by John McDermott with Eddie Kramer (Warner Books, New York, 1994)

Hendrix: The Visual Documentary by Tony Brown (Omnibus Press, London, 1992)

Jimi Hendrix: Electric Gypsy by Harry Shapiro & Caesar Glebbeek (St. Martin's Press, New York, 1995)

The Jimi Hendrix Experience by Jerry Hopkins (Plexus, London, 1996)

Jimi Hendrix in His Own Words by Tony Brown (Omnibus Press, London, 1994)

Jimi Hendrix: Inside the Experience by Mitch Mitchell & John Platt (St. Martin's Press, New York, 1994)

Jimi Hendrix Sessions by John McDermott, Billy Cox, and Eddie Kramer et al (Little, Brown, and Company, New York, 1995)

'Scuse Me While I Kiss the Sky by David Henderson (Omnibus Press, London, 1990)

Through Gypsy Eyes by Kathy Etchingham (Victor Gollancz, London, 1998)

index

Figures in italics indicate photographs. Main references to songs are in bold type.